MW00824689

Johansen Skovsted

© 2024 Verlag der Buchhandlung Walther und Franz König, Cologne

Director and Editor of *2G* Moisés Puente
Graphic design RafamateoStudio
Proofreading George Hutton
Cover photograph Rasmus Norlander
Lithography Rovira Digital, Barcelona
Print agpograf impressors, Barcelona

All rights reserved. No part of this publication may be produced, stored in a retrieval system or transmitted in any form or by any means, electronic, mechanical, photocopying, recording or otherwise, without the prior permission of the publisher.

First published by
Verlag der Buchhandlung Walther und Franz König
Ehrenstrasse 4
D-50672 Köln
verlag@buchhandlung-walther-koenig.de

Printed in Spain
ISBN: 978-3-7533-0478-6

Distribution

Germany, Austria and Switzerland
Buchhandlung Walther König, Cologne
Tel. +49 (0) 221 / 20 59 6-53
Fax +49 (0) 221 / 20 59 6-60
verlag@buchhandlung-walther-koenig.de

Distribution outside the United States and Canada, Germany, Austria and Switzerland
Thames & Hudson Ltd., London
www.thamesandhudson.com

United States and Canada
D.A.P. / Distributed Art Publishers, Inc., New York
www.artbook.com

Contents

Logistics

On a grey August morning, Søren Johansen and Sebastian Skovsted drove me towards the outskirts of Køge, a Danish town. It had been raining heavily, and the clouds were still hanging low. We went past randomly scattered warehouses, dull office buildings, residential areas full of "catalogue houses, typical of Denmark" (as Søren put it), as well as some vast, empty plots.

Traffic was quiet on the large, smooth roads. I saw only a handful of lorries, and a few cars. Most people were still on their summer holidays. Soon, though, Denmark would go back to work.

We were heading for the recently completed CODAN Office and Warehouse, by Johansen Skovsted Arkitekter. CODAN is a major manufacturer of hospital equipment, including syringes and infusion sets (many

Philip Ursprung is Professor of the History of Art and Architecture at the Department of Architecture at ETH Zurich. From 2017 to 2019, he served as Dean of the Department. He is editor of *Herzog & de Meuron: Natural History* (2002) and author of *Allan Kaprow, Robert Smithson, and the Limits to Art* (2013); *Brechas y conexiones* (2016); *Der Wert der Oberfläche* (2017); *Representation of Labor / Performative Historiography* (2018); *Joseph Beuys: Kunst Kapital Revolution* (2021); he is also co-editor of *Gordon Matta-Clark: An Archival Sourcebook* (2022). In 2023, he is representing Switzerland, alongside Karin Sander, at the Venice Biennale of Architecture, with the exhibition *Neighbours*.

of us are likely to have been jabbed by one of their syringes, for the Covid-19 vaccine). The company's directors commissioned Johansen Skovsted Arkitekter to design their new building, as one of the first within its particular zoning area. This part of the country has been earmarked to become Denmark's main transportation and logistics hub; the specific area next to the hospital is dedicated to the healthcare industry.

Among the sprawl of generic infrastructure buildings, the CODAN complex immediately caught my eye. The greenish-grey structure, assembled from prefabricated concrete slabs, has a strong presence. It was as if someone had adjusted a lens, bringing a blurred image into focus. The surfaces of the concrete slabs alternate between a smooth and rough texture. The concrete's aggregate consists of Norwegian calcite, which produces a subtle glittering effect. The edges of the slabs are pale green in colour.

The nuanced design heightens the impression of relief. In line with the building regulations, it is just two storeys high, and its overall appearance is that of a massive, quasi-sculptural construction (not boxlike, as with most warehouses). Rather than being completely out-of-scale and towering over humans, it relates to the size of the human body. I immediately wanted to touch the façade with my fingers.

The warehouse reminded me of an actor who appears on stage but remains silent for a while before speaking. But what's the story behind the building? In short, logistics are a driver of economic growth: the rapid and cheap movement of standardised shipping containers has profoundly changed life in industrialised societies. However, container ships and truck convoys are major polluters, and the closure of city-centre department stores — along with the increasing number of warehouses being built in the peripheries — is disrupting urban structures. The Covid-19 pandemic underlined the vulnerability of international supply lines; the CODAN warehouse is a result of the obligation to ensure that sufficient medical supplies can reach Danish clients and hospitals.

Despite the fact that containers, trucks and warehouses are part of a powerful system, they are strangely formless. They are both omnipresent and invisible. There are certain rare, iconic exceptions, such as the Ricola Storage Building in Laufen, Switzerland, built in the late 1980s by Herzog & de Meuron; or the Sedus High-Bay Warehouse in Dogern, Germany, by Sauerbruch Hutton, built in the early 2000s. Generally speaking, though, warehouses are nondescript sheds, of no interest to architects. With the CODAN warehouse, Johansen Skovsted mediate between the human scale and the network of logistics: they seek to give logistics an aesthetic, a face, a story, a narrative.

Care

To give logistics a face is one challenge for architecture. Another challenge is that of the architectural representation of healthcare. The healthcare industries are booming too, but, like logistics, they have no recognisable face. A century ago, medical and architectural progress were profoundly intertwined: that is, the aesthetic norms of Modernist architecture — with its whiteness, purity, transparency and rationality — were deeply linked to notions around hygiene, fresh air, clear daylight and smooth surfaces (they were also linked to the racist and colonialist ideology of the supposed superiority of white Europeans, one should add).

Like many architects of their generation, Johansen Skovsted question this highly ambivalent legacy. The hygiene norms for the CODAN building are of course strict: ceilings need to be easily dusted, and floors easily cleaned. Temperature changes must be kept to a minimum. However, as I entered the building, I did not feel controlled; I sensed a welcoming, almost domestic atmosphere. Absent are the usual modernist residues: there is no whiteness here, no chrome or polished surfaces, no glass doors or large office spaces or homogenous lighting. Instead, I perceived soft, moderate colours such as light green and grey, with wood, nuances and contrasts. The ceiling height varies. Rather than huge, open-plan offices, the workers have individual spaces where doors can be closed. The windows are low, which invites workers to sit down, while also making the office spaces appear higher than they actually are. Johansen Skovsted even designed the large meeting tables.

Unlike in many new concrete buildings, the acoustics are good. We automatically lowered our voices. Furthermore, the amount of care taken for the workers' wellbeing becomes patently clear in the warehouse. Skylights bring in daylight, and a large window connects to the outside. I was reminded of the use of natural light in buildings by Louis I. Kahn, and the scenography of Adolphe Appia. The newly planted surroundings, with flowers, grass, shrubs and young trees, are easily accessible. Rather than a factory, the layout recalls a monastery: a central, refectory-like dining room serves as a meeting place, while a densely planted cloister-like courtyard both separates and connects the directors' offices from those of the staff. In sum, the atmosphere is not sterile, but fertile. As we left the site, I plucked an apple from one of the newly planted trees.

Horizon

Seen from a Swiss perspective, Denmark is incredibly flat, with a very broad horizon. The topography here was smoothed out by glaciers during the last Ice Age, and its contours continue to be shaped and reshaped by the sediments of river deltas and the movements of sandy coasts. The landscape is now, at least partially, a man-made environment, due to the deforestation that began in Medieval times, along with the 20th-century meliorations and the recent rise of infrastructure buildings for renewable energy. The human and non-human intertwine. "Nature" can only be thought of with inverted commas.

We joined the highway, heading west via the spectacular Storebæltsbro, the Great Belt Bridge, which connects the islands of Zealand and Fyn. It opened 25 years ago, and was designed by the Danish firm Dissing+Weitling; it is one of the longest suspension bridges in the world. Whilst we took in the elegant structure and breathtaking view, Sebastian and Søren told me of their fascination with infrastructure buildings. They had visited booming China in the early 2000s, when they were students, and the experience left a lasting impression on them.

Sebastian and Søren studied at the Royal Danish Academy in Copenhagen. As an architectural school, traditionally it was (and still is) more like an art school than a technical university. For a while they taught at the Academy's Institute for Architecture and Technology, and they are in constant exchange with engineers and technicians. They have close ties to art too. Along with the artist Lea Porsager, they designed Anatta House for dOCUMENTA (13) in 2012. They also participated in the travelling exhibition *Alternative Histories*, contributing a model based on a drawing by Peter Märkli. In Rasmus Norlander, they have found a photographer whose carefully structured analogue images depict buildings in relation to their environment, in a way that precisely gets across the architects' formal intentions. Like many architects trained in Europe around the turn of the millennium, Søren and Sebastian combine the two souls of architecture: that of the Beaux-Arts, and that of engineering.

We passed the outskirts of Odense before crossing another bridge that led us to Jutland, the Danish mainland. The further west we went, the less densely populated the land became. It was almost the opposite of the bustling Copenhagen-Malmö area where our journey had started. There were no warehouses anymore, just the occasional barn or stable. No lorries, just tractors. No empty construction sites, but vast fields with corn and wheat, and some pastures with cows and sheep. The farmhouses here were large, a result of the widespread transformation and intensification of the agricultural industry, typical across the European Union. I was reminded that Denmark was once a mainly agricultural country. Today, the primary sector of the economy — fishing, agriculture, mining — is almost negligible in comparison with the country's tertiary sector. As a consequence, many small towns and villages in western Denmark are struggling with economic decline and depopulation: here, wind turbines for generating electric energy are soaring in number, but railway stations and post offices stand empty.

Birds

As we approached the coast, the clouds went away and the sun blazed in the blue sky. We left the asphalt road and turned onto a gravel path. I enjoyed the vast horizon, the wind coming from the lagoon, the smell of the heathland. In an attempt to activate the local tourism industry, the Danish Nature Agency and Realdania launched an initiative to make a bird sanctuary accessible, at the tip of the peninsula of the Ringkøbing Fjord. The sanctuary was founded almost a century ago, and is an important breeding ground for migratory birds. Johansen Skovsted were commissioned to renovate the house where the ornithologists stay, and also design an observation tower, a hide and a workshop and toilet building. This complex is used by professional birdwatchers, as well as the other visitors who are allowed in at certain times of the year.

The migrant birds had not yet arrived on their way south, so we were allowed to access the site. From afar, the tower came into view. I'd seen it in the photographs by Rasmus Norlander; to date, it is the most iconic structure that Johansen Skovsted have ever designed, and I was eager to see it in person. Again, it was as if someone had adjusted a lens. "Does it look taller than you imagined?", Sebastian asked. It is roughly five storeys high, about thirteen metres. It is assembled entirely out of galvanised iron sheets and iron bars; it appears both robust and fragile, heavy and light. Its top is wider than its base. The uppermost platform is used both by professional ornithologists and hobby photographers or tourists. It is covered by a metal roof, and can be closed with translucent fibreglass sheets to shield those inside from wind and rain. Unlike the CODAN building, I found it hard to relate the size of the observation tower to the human scale; I struggled to answer Sebastian's question. Just like earlier, when I was standing in front of the CODAN building, I couldn't help but think of an actor appearing on stage.

What's the story of this observation tower in Tipperne? Its presence is rooted in its very ambiguity — it is simultaneously a tower and a cage. It avoids the typology of traditional watchtowers, those which invariably evoke the idea of a prison, a camp, a fire lookout tower or a box stand for hunting, all of which taper at the top and have a large footprint. Furthermore, structures like that are normally divided in two, i.e. a space to observe and a ladder to climb. Johansen Skovsted's tower avoids this hierarchy: rather than separating the climbing and the watching, the two actions here are indivisible. That is, throughout the whole process of going up the tower, those inside can view the landscape and the birds. Every element of the construction is essential, for reasons of statics, safety and function. A handrail adds further stability to the structure, while the metal bars bear the load and prevent visitors from falling.

The tower corresponds to the way birds use space — constantly moving in three dimensions, and defying gravity. This partly explains why the architects designed a structure that has neither a typical top nor a typical foot (it has a small footprint and hardly seems to touch the fragile ground, although, in reality, it is anchored with a massive, invisible concrete foundation). Depending on the light, it can be difficult to make out the volume of the construction. On a hazy winter day, it might even resemble a drawing.

Folly

Ornithologists focus mainly on birds that are breeding — they define the species they see, and they count individual birds and the number of eggs. This tower gives them a good view of the breeding grounds. The client also asked for a hide, mainly aimed at tourists. Again, the architects chose to use metal (in this case Corten steel sheets) rather than wood; the rust colour blends into the landscape, providing some degree of camouflage. Visitors can enter the space and watch through a narrow opening. Inside, they stand slightly above the ground, on a metal platform (there is an additional metal sheet specially designed for children). Unlike the viewing tower, the hide does not follow strictly functional criteria: it is, instead, a device that enhances aesthetic perception. Whereas, normally, a hide should be almost invisible, Johansen Skovsted opted to make it stand out, which also helps with orientation in this flat landscape. Its shape, or figure, however, is unlike anything else in the area. For me, it brought to mind sculptures by Richard Serra, Alexander Graham Bell's tetrahedral kites, a meteorological station or one of Olafur Eliasson's early viewing installations.

The four figures — house, tower, hide and shed — are markers that articulate the landscape, besides their individual functions for birdwatching. Johansen Skovsted deliberately chose to differentiate the structures. In fact, they look as if they had been designed by four different authors. Each figure is unique and specific; they are not variations on a theme. Had they spoken one architectural language, the effect would have been different: as structures, they would have looked like elements of a coherent system that measures, controls and colonises the ground. I was reminded of Christopher Alexander's concept of the organic environment, where "every place is unique, and the different places also cooperate, with no parts left over, to create a global whole — a whole which can be identified by everyone who is part of it".[1]

Pumphouse

The bird sanctuary is part of the Skjern River Delta. This area had been meliorated in the 20th century in order to gain arable land, but, since the early 2000s, it has now been restored. Three pump stations, designed by Myhrwold and Rasmussen from the mid-1960s, remain steadfast as testimonies of society's earlier attempts at dominating nature; that melioration destroyed much of the local biodiversity. Now that the agrarian industry is shrinking, and tourism is booming, the delta itself is considered the major attraction. Some of the pumps still operate to regulate the water level, and they now also serve as viewpoints and information centres for tourists.

Johansen Skovsted were commissioned to transform three pump stations. Near the Pump Station North, we passed a cluster of hunting cabins (bird-hunting seems to be more popular in the area than birdwatching). Groups of tourists came to the

1 — Alexander, Christopher, *et. al.*, *The Oregon Experiment*, New York: Oxford University Press, 1975, p. 11.

pump station by bike. I was surprised to see how much care the original designers and builders, back in the 1960s, had taken with these infrastructure buildings. There is a well-balanced play of groove concrete and brick, as if those architects, half a century ago, had somehow suspected that one day their constructions would be seen not only by a handful of technicians adjusting the pumps, but also by visitors coming to enjoy the landscape.

Johansen Skovsted left the existing structures almost as found. The old pumps remain. Any fragile equipment was covered by wooden panels. Window frames and metal doors were painted green. The immediate environment — previously marked by tall fences, lampposts and a clutter of signs and warnings — has been cleared, and there is now a narrow fence for safety reasons. The pump station is accessible and welcoming. There are no traces of the "no access" and "danger" signs that traditionally protect such devices. Simply put, they left everything as found, and opened a door. The opening, which was originally used for bringing in machinery, has been transformed into a spectacular panoramic window.

The rooftop terrace is accessible via a stairwell and a lift, and it offers a striking view of the river delta. Johansen Skovsted added wooden structures. From a distance, this addition looks as if it had always been there; the wooden structures provide shelter, but more importantly they are a frame, a device to observe and sharpen one's gaze. The mounting of the battens echoes the rhythm of the grooved concrete surface. The wooden installation allows visitors to experience the different views.

Visitor centres lie in that tricky ground between scenography and exhibition architecture, so they pose a challenge to architects. With the Pump Station North, Johansen Skovsted again manage to give a face to this category, while also dealing, sensitively, with a building of industrial heritage. Rather than just conserving it as a museum, they transform it into to a hybrid that serves both purposes, namely operation and viewing.

Resonance

As we started our drive back to Copenhagen, the sun was still high in the sky. The light was golden and the shadows grew longer, typical of Scandinavian summer days. Is Johansen Skovsted's architecture specifically "Danish", "Scandinavian" or "Nordic"? It's hard to draw a line between national schools or styles at a time when education, technology and building materials have become largely internationalised. Johansen Skovsted avoid typologies and the repetition of clichés, but there are certain cultural specificities that do resonate in their projects. As I stepped down from the concrete porch of the CODAN office and onto the sandy ground, which was covered in grass and flowers, I recalled Copenhagen's key role in combining urban development and landscape design — an effort that was in fact acknowledged when the city came to be declared the UNESCO-UIA World Capital of Architecture for 2023. As I walked along the soft ground of Tipperne, on what used to be a seabed, I thought of the pioneering leadership of Denmark with regards to environmental protection; it was one of the first countries to establish a Ministry for the Environment, back in the early 1970s. And as I stood on the pump station, observing nature retaking the formerly regulated swamps, I thought of the famous Danish restaurant NOMA (the acronym refers to "Nordic" and "food") and the way it combines high-tech methods with very locally-sourced produce.

It was dark when we got to Copenhagen. In my imagination, the impressions of the day were mixing with Rasmus Norlander's photographs. Many of these images focus on landscapes, half natural, half shaped by human intervention. The ambivalence of the land is absorbed in Johansen Skovsted's work. Their careful observation of details — as well as their mediation between the human and the non-human, the natural and the industrial — is exemplary, even beyond the realm of Nordic architecture. There is much to learn from their approach. The industrial, be it logistics, healthcare or tourism, both improves and diminishes the quality of daily life; it is profitable to some, a loss to others. Johansen Skovsted's buildings accept and articulate this ambiguity. Looking at the skylight in an office space, one suddenly notices the raw edge of the concrete slab. Entering the fragile hide, one is reminded of the immense force of the nearby North Sea. Contemplating the idyll outside the pump station, one is interrupted by the splashing of the pumps underfoot. Johansen Skovsted's buildings make us perceive internal contradiction. Rather than reducing tensions, they allow them to unfold and resonate.

Tent Poles in the Ground
Stephen Bates

I have a copy of a sketch by José Antonio Coderch from around 1951; it is part of the field notes he made while walking the site of what would become the Ugalde House. The drawing consists of pencil points that demarcate the position of specific trees, along with circled numbers, dimensions describing heights, other scribbled notes — like "vista estupenda desde α a β" (great view from α towards β) — and dashed lines that seem to indicate something of the topography of the ground. In this sketch, Coderch is bringing together his key observations that would inform his evolving idea for a house that was radically organic in character, becoming part of the landscape. Coderch was 38, and at a formative stage in his career. This sketch comes to my mind when reflecting on the work of Søren Johansen and Sebastian Skovsted, who are, as I write, only a few years older than Coderch at the time of the Ugalde House, and in an equally

Stephen Bates graduated from the Royal College of Art, London, in 1989. He gained professional experience in London and Barcelona before establishing Sergison Bates with Jonathan Sergison in 1996.
He has taught at a number of schools of architecture, including the Architectural Association in London, ETH Zurich, EPF Lausanne, ESARQ and ETSAB in Barcelona, the Oslo School of Architecture, GSD Harvard and the University of Antwerp. Since 2009, he has been Professor of Urbanism and Housing at the Technical University of Munich.

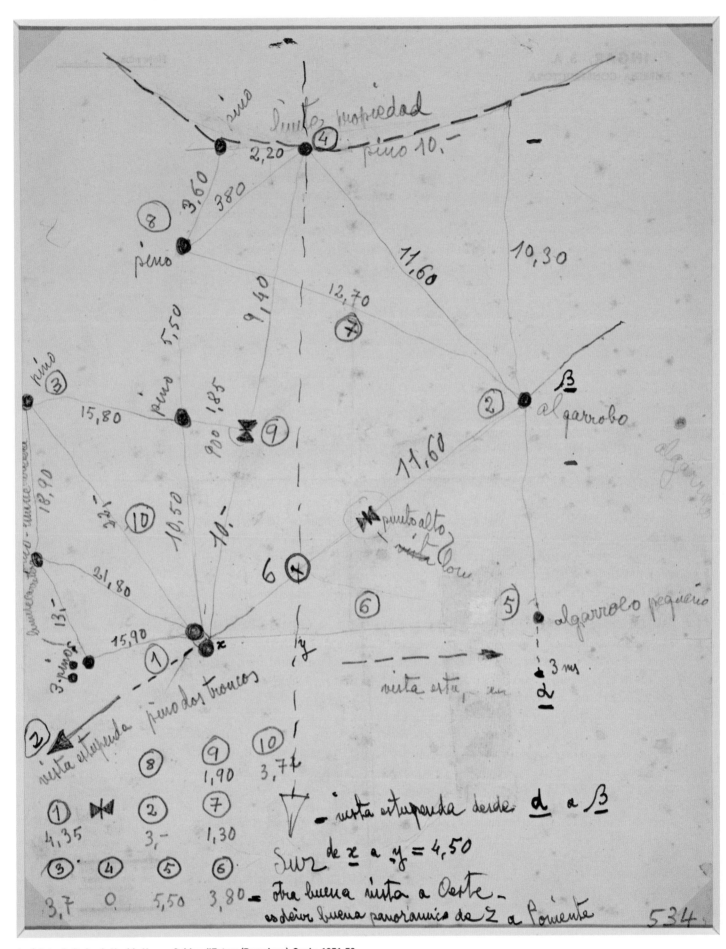

José Antonio Coderch, Ugalde House, Caldes d'Estrac (Barcelona), Spain, 1951-52.
Survey of the terrain with the position of the tree trunks.
© Museo Nacional Centro de Arte Reina Sofía, Madrid

formative phase of their creative lives. I have always enjoyed that sketch, not just as a record of the creative process, but also for what it represents, i.e. the architect marking the ground, as with tent poles, staking out a territory of places to work on, and in-between spaces where to linger. The poles indicate a line of thought: marking out new poles — or moving those which were previously important and now feel less so — records the evolution of one's work, as it gains momentum in the process of thinking, then making, reflecting, then making again.

Coderch was, to borrow Alison and Peter Smithson's words, one of the "silent architects" who are defined by what they do rather than what they say. Such architects are, "by the complexity of invention [,] unaware of doing", and it is precisely what they are unable to talk about that "shifts the tide of architecture".[1] As with other certain architects — Sigurd Lewerentz, Dimitris Pikionis, Konstantin Melnikov, Charles and Ray Eames, Max Bill — Coderch's quiet, self-effacing work lay at the margins of architectural debate, despite its great originality and significance; upon re-evaluation, it could change our view of the present and re-adjust our understanding of the past. I would add Jørn Utzon to the count: his work has been fundamental to the expression of Danish architectural culture since the 1970s, and has perhaps had even more of an influence on the emerging architects of this millennium. His use of precast industrial and hand-made elements exemplified the process of assimilation and reinterpretation, a process at the heart of a conscious engagement with local knowledge and materials within a globalised context. Utzon's work epitomises what Kenneth Frampton defined as the aim of critical regionalism, that is, an architecture with "an expressive density and resonance" that embodies the specific culture of a particular place in an intentional way.[2]

We talk about this as we embark on a field trip around West Jutland and Copenhagen to visit Johansen Skovsted's recent work, for they too occupy this small world of architectural thought that crosses boundaries and sometimes generations — a web of references, conversations and friendships that help stake out those tent poles and develop an architectural position through practice. Johansen and Skovsted talk of their collaborations with other young European architects, like Veldhuis from Brussels, and their teaching exchanges with Clancy Moore from Dublin, as well as Rodrigo da Costa Lima and Amélia Brandao Costa, founders of the Porto Academy. In this sense, although their work to date is located in Denmark, it is inextricably linked to a wider European platform of ideas.

Søren Johansen (1981) and Sebastian Skovsted (1982) met as architecture students at the Royal Danish Academy in Copenhagen. The school has gained a significant reputation in recent years, since the introduction in 2012 of the Master's Programme, led by Christoffer Harlang, at the Department of Cultural Heritage, Transformation and Conservation (KTR). Harlang and his teaching partner, Nicolai Bo Andersen, together with other researchers — among them Erik Brandt Dam, who taught Johansen and Skovsted as undergraduates — have refocussed the school's agenda towards

1 — Smithson, Alison and Peter, "The Silent Architects", in VV. AA., *Sigurd Lewerentz: 1885-1975: The Dilemma of Classicism*, London: Architectural Association, 1989.

2 — Frampton, Kenneth, "Towards a Critical Regionalism: Six Points for an Architecture of Resistance," in Hal Foster (ed.), *The Anti-Aesthetic: Essays on Postmodern Culture*, Port Townsend: Bay Press, 1983

sustainability, regionalism and materiality. Through courses structured around seminars on joinery, stone masonry and metal casting, they have encouraged the re-learning of craft forms and techniques which are at risk of disappearing and have long been neglected by architects. Many of the teachers who later joined the KTR were already teaching at the Academy as Johansen and Skovsted were studying, and they both acknowledge the important role these teachers played in shifting the conversation from geometrical abstraction and the making of iconic images to engaging more meaningfully with material building culture.

Having committed to working in practice together, Johansen and Skovsted pursued parallel learning paths: Johansen trained with Jens Bertelsen (Bertelsen & Scheving Arkitekter) in Copenhagen, and Skovsted with architecten de vylder vinck taillieu (advvt) in Ghent, Belgium. They found time to work together on speculative projects and competitions during the in-between hours of office practice.

As I walked with them around their built work, ten years or so later — an opportunity to experience the materiality of their projects, listen to the way they speak about their work (sometimes finishing each other's sentences), look at their construction and presentation drawings — their profound understanding of the discipline of architecture became readily apparent. Their projects are rooted in a thorough study of the spatiality, cultural significance and materiality of the pre-existing situation, which captures the "soul" of the project and steers the design. They follow a dialectical process; the strategy of the project informs the detail, and the detail feeds back to reinforce the strategy. What the architects call "creative obstacles" — the constraints of brief and place, together with their own ambitions — create a framework for thinking and decision-making that is specific to each project.

This way of working entails an equally conscious approach to the presentation of the finished work. Johansen and Skovsted's long-term collaboration with Swedish photographer Rasmus Norlander has established a distinctive character for the representation of their work and how it is experienced through photographs. Norlander uses a large-format camera, as well as traditional exposure and developing techniques, so his photography is purposefully analogue in its presentation. The buildings come to rest within large, desaturated landscapes, and they appear as autonomous objects, often enfolded by the mist of surrounding space. Norlander's photography is completely apt for their finished projects to date, and it will be interesting to see how this representation evolves as the architects' work shifts in scale and becomes more urban, the context more complex and multi-layered. However, what is striking — and in my view crucial for an evolving practice — is that they have developed a strong working methodology through years of intense collaborative thinking. As I watch them sitting side by side, sketching together onto a single drawing, their ongoing conversation becomes manifest in lines and marks. I feel I am witnessing the setting out of those tent poles, the stage where ideas become imprinted and absorbed, the roots of their continuing development, a point of orientation as their relationship evolves, as any creative partnership must.

Johansen Skovsted Arkitekter, pump
station transformation, Skjern River,
Denmark, 2015.
Photo: © Stephen Bates

As we experience this architecture and talk about it while driving, while walking
and eating together, certain themes of investigation become discernible. These
themes structure certain ideas that frame the work and recur across projects in
the form of strategies, or simply as interests that become evident. I point out these
observations in passing, and they are sometimes met with a faint smile, sometimes
with surprise, often with a studied nod of appreciation.

Structure and Lattice

The rooftop extension to the Pump Station North on the Skjern River is constructed in carpentry, consisting of two triangular frames: a closed one, accommodating
stair and lift, and another one open to the sides, but covered. As it is a cold structure, there is freedom available in the sculptural and spatial possibilities of the
joinery. This is when I first notice that Johansen and Skovsted tend to work without
hierarchy between cladding and structure: the timber sections, laid flat or rotated
as fins to form an intricate lattice of woven elements, are simultaneously surface,
load-bearing, and bracing structure. The timber planks' verticality rhymes with
the order of the existing host building's profiled concrete wall panels, which were

cast *in situ*. With weathering, the patina on both has merged the additions and the host building to form a newly re-vitalised whole. The delicacy of the rooftop lightens the mass of the original pump station, giving it a new outline against the big skies. It now offers a public viewing platform over the vast landscape of the river delta between Tarm and Skjern — a place to rest, somewhere simply to be.

The lattice is an artwork that cannot be described in merely functional terms: it is a clearly studied visual composition, and an expression of materiality and making that involved the carpenters on site. I see evidence of this interest in other projects: the smaller ones often seem to be prototypes for future work, or for developing an idea further, having tested it beforehand. The brass shelving made for the Marienborg residence of the Danish Prime Minister, for example, employs the lattice of standard brass profiles as an open shelving rack in the library, and as a sideboard in the sitting room. Johansen and Skovsted worked with a local blacksmith to develop a system of proportion and structure: it had gradual increments in vertical proportions and horizontal profile offsets, thus creating a complex lattice of elements where repetition is difficult to perceive. The result is a delicate "breathing" structure, made from the same 15 × 15 mm brass profiles throughout.

Johansen Skovsted Arkitekter, Bird sanctuary (tower), Tipperne, Denmark, 2017.
Photo: © Stephen Bates

This interest in using all parts of the structure for load-bearing purposes is also evident in the Tipperne birdwatching tower, which overlooks the Ringkøbing Fjord. Here, the solid-section galvanised steel bars form a protective lattice that carries the site's forces through the structure, creating a protective cage and balustrading. All the steel elements carry the forces of compression and tension. Although this project has come to define the practice, following its widespread international exposure and Norlander's iconic photography, it is only when you stand in front of it and climb up inside it that you understand how it relates to its surroundings. The tower echoes nearby navigation beacons, weather stations and tall three-legged sea markers with their poles and cables, and it rests delicately on the ground against the strong prevailing wind that sweeps across the open landscape and shallow waters of the Fjord.

This interest in bringing structure and cladding together as a conglomerate whole can also be seen in the CODAN office and warehouse project in Køge. There, a standard prefabricated concrete system is customised to provide a spatial shell, lined where necessary — in the working spaces — and left exposed in the storage areas.

Sameness and Proportion

CODAN Companies — a successful manufacturer and distributor of medical devices, well known for the injection moulding of essential infusion components — is a family-run business. Despite the company's international reach, there is still a strong sense of a personal, non-corporate attitude toward making spaces for work and distribution, which is evinced by the architecture. Using a prefabricated construction system seems an obvious choice, both in terms of the context — an out-of-town business park — and the programme. Johansen and Skovsted describe an instinct to select a material or a system, and then explore its potential to find form. It is an expedient response that allows them to be open to conceptualising the construction itself.

The system of implied pilasters and over panels, described in subtle relief, gives the elevations a strong presence. A closer look reveals gaps between elements that result in a gentle "floating" of planes, emphasised by the combination of smooth finishes on some parts, and coarser, aggregated finishes on others. A discernible pilaster is described by the precast relief measuring 220 × 52 cm, with a corresponding recess of coarse finish above, and a smooth over-panel of 195 × 185 cm between. The composition gives a median line just off centre to the elevation, and a pleasing just-off-square vertical proportion to the window opening at ground-floor level and panel above. It is elegant, beautiful in my eyes, and it gets better as you move around the building; the system adapts to the volumetric demands of the programme behind the façade. As the façade steps to enfold the warehouse, the proportional scale of the pilasters and panels adapts incrementally to form a stacked composition. Much is achieved by the contrast of rough and smooth finishes, the exposed aggregate of pale Norwegian marble ennobling the standard prefabricated system.

Transforming ordinary components and systems is another noticeable tendency in the work of Johansen Skovsted, and there is evidence everywhere of how they manipulate the potential of the prefabricated system to provide specific answers to different situations: this is apparent in their treatment of the various scales, in how they make porches, or how they integrate service doors and generous openings. The precast panel system — part of the language of 1960s architecture, invented to allow the efficient repetition of elements — is here turned on its head to make a vast number of specific and varied elements. We talk about how prefabrication suggests an exact repetition: it removes specific expressions of use and idiosyncrasies of place in favour of standardisation. In turn, this often results in a deadening of the façade's energy, and we agree about the potential in variation within "sameness". Sameness is a strategic concept which is experiential and tolerant, rigorous in expression, yet loose and adaptable: it can be modified to suit a place, use or way of life. In architecture, sameness reconciles industrialising ambitions and human-scale ideas of proportion and hierarchy, as well as the ability to adapt to the specifics of place and tolerances of on-site construction.

On the south side of the building, where the plan unfolds to form a planted courtyard surrounded by office spaces, the system is exposed to framing beams and columns made from the same extruded profile as elements found elsewhere. When you enter directly from an office or a communal hall into the loggia formed by these elements, it is a striking moment: the view to the garden foreground is framed against the backdrop of a wild meadow. In this space, another important component of the prefabricated system becomes visible, namely the painted steel connecting plate that provides transitional linkage between horizontal and vertical planes. The plates are used throughout the building, although they are generally discernible only as shadows in recesses. They allow the system to be presented as a set of rather delicate prefabricated pieces, avoiding the bulking-up of the section at points of torsion. In the loggia, they become an overt part of the composition, forming visual "knots" at the junction of symbolic posts (narrow precast extrusions) and symbolic beams (matching extrusions). The plates visually reinforce the thin, delicate framing of elements.

Pavilion and Territory

On our field trip, a lot of our time is spent "in the field", in and around the buildings resting in the landscape — and the landscape itself is often the protagonist. There is great sympathy for nature in Johansen Skovsted's work, which involves important collaborations with landscape designers. At CODAN, the wild meadow to the south of the building, with its natural water attenuation marshland, was designed together with Marianne Levinsen. Here, landscape is presented as a found space rather than an overtly manmade composition, an instinct which I am sure is deeply embedded in Danish culture. The first work I saw — from a distance, as we drove by — was the Pump Station East, which looked like a ruin in the landscape, a fragment of a much broader territory of agricultural and reclaimed land. It was a reminder of the omnipresence of landscape in West Jutland, and the work required to manage it and make it productive. The Bagges Dam, constructed in 1865 to secure the area from the water of the fjord, was followed by various land management measures, including the straightening of the Skjern River in the 1960s and the draining of 4,000 hectares of bog and meadow which were converted to intensive agricultural land. The pump stations are the remnants of the municipality's draining programme, and their re-appropriation by Johansen Skovsted has made them publicly accessible, but has also made the stillness of the landscape more palpable. Views from each station are like still lifes, framed by openings, reminiscent of the landscape paintings by Harald Møller, P. C. Skovgaard, Johan Thomas Lundbye and Vilhelm Hammershøi.

The idea of a building as ruin, or as a pavilion in the landscape, is most pronounced at Tipperne. Here, the birdwatching tower is the pavilion and the bird-hide is the ruin; the latter is a folded Corten tent-like form poking out from the heather, like an upturned boat run aground. The tower — which was originally intended to be positioned further away from the neighbouring buildings (it is now just twenty metres from them, the maximum distance allowed by the Landscape Agency) — retains a certain remoteness, creating an experience of solitude within the landscape.

Local and Universal

Each project is deeply embedded in its context, while also embodying a search for universal ideas of form. Johansen Skovsted's work connects easily with the ambitions of a critical regionalism and the work of their compatriot Jørn Utzon, in the way it assimilates and reinterprets universal ideas in a local context. The modular assembly of welded cages that form the stepped outline of the Tipperne tower has a hand-made quality of finish. The triangular plan is made up of four sliding galvanised panels on each side, one of them translucent, combined with three hinged glass screens that block the wind. It was originally designed around sight lines, to allow the very specific movement and adjustment of a telescope which has since been removed. And yet, despite no longer serving its original purpose, the structure retains a sense of usefulness: the strong plan form and components make it feel specific to its place, and yet somehow archetypal. The diagonal reappears in the Pump Station North, dividing the rooftop space into four segments in the most direct way, and framing those conical views of the landscape, heightened by a considered use of colour.

Patina and Paint

The bright orange paint, as used on some faces of the timber lattice, gives depth and nuance to the screen: it is transformed from something reminiscent of an agricultural fence into a sculptural installation of sorts. The orange contrasts pleasantly with the grey patination of the timber, the weathered ribbed concrete below it and the green landscape beyond, and is accentuated by the verdigris on the lattice at the Pump Station South. Johansen Skovsted see colour as an important part of their repertoire. I am reminded of Per Kirkeby, who maintained that colours have meaning and properties, though these are often difficult to make out. The subtle green wash applied to the smooth surfaces of the concrete panels at CODAN removes the grey of the cement, giving it a softer tint, complemented by the pale green of the window frames, ceiling soffits and service doors. These subtleties change the mood of the project: a place that could easily feel rather cold, solely focused on industrial production, becomes something more delicate, more inviting. This colour strategy continues into the interior.

Rooms and Carpets

The plan at CODAN establishes a set of halls placed on a path that leads through the building. The halls are identified by their height and by a mat of green floor tiles along the way. They are common rooms, places of exchange, change of direction, giving options and access to different parts of the programme. We talk over a nice drawing made explicitly to describe the spatial strategy. Rooms are important in Johansen Skovsted's work, and this is evident in their most recent project, the house at Laveskov. The floor plan of the house is laid out on a single level, and is a cluster of eleven adjoining rooms linked by openings on the corners, thereby setting up multiple diagonal views and routes. The threshold between them is of-

Johansen Skovsted Arkitekter, CODAN, Køge, Denmark, 2023.
Photo: © Stephen Bates

ten given spatial depth by incorporating storage within the door assemblies. With doors left generally open in everyday use, the thresholds create subtle shadow spaces between rooms, which are lit with a variety of directional light. Sometimes the window can be seen from a distance, with a long view out to sea, but often it is only the evidence of light on the floor that you experience. The plan encourages movement through and between, and the floors of soft sand-coloured bricks or pale spruce boards differentiate the character of the rooms. Around the perimeter of this internal cluster, three satellite rooms, like pavilions set apart from the main volume, create small yards in the in-between spaces. They are perhaps the most exquisite part of this plan and remind me of the gentle gap-spaces at Can Lis. While this is a home for a specific client, it is also a speculation about how to live, the cellular plan offering appropriation and creating a non-hierarchical domestic proposal that is relevant to the current debate on collective living.

Tent Poles

At CODAN, the shape of a droplet — made with stainless steel formwork and produced in the company's own workshop — is cast into eleven of the concrete panels, and discreetly arranged around the building, both inside and out. You come across the droplets by chance, an intimate encounter with the building and a reminder of the owners' ethos. This instinct to mark the building — to make it personal and specific, and allow it to be "perfectly imperfect" — is at the heart of Johansen Skovsted's work. It is a crucial element in a critical practice intent on finding a synthesis between local and universal culture, about place and circumstance, about atmospheres and experiences. Like those aforementioned silent architects (who remain constant mentors to those of us who inhabit this same small world), Johansen and Skovsted are on a journey of discovery from one project to another. It will be interesting to watch as they continue to stake out the tent poles in front of them, working things out by thinking, then making, reflecting, then making again.

Johansen Skovsted Arkitekter, CODAN, Køge, Denmark, 2023.
Droplet in a concrete panel.
Photo: © Stephen Bates

Transformation of Nørrehus courtyard, Copenhagen

2014-16

This project, commissioned by the homeowners' association of the Nørrehus apartment complex, transformed the residents' courtyard: before, it was a purely utilitarian space with large paved areas, and it was to be reoriented towards leisure and community. The first stage worked on all the surfaces, new planting and playground. The second phase dealt with a new house for the common facilities, including room for prams, the housekeeper, as well as waste and recycling.

The transformation of the courtyard landscape and the new utility building was financed by the surplus on the housing association's maintenance budget, and was only feasible because reutilisation and existing elements were the key design parameters. By removing run-down paved areas, and replacing them with green surfaces, repair costs were minimised. The existing drainage and wells were left untouched, so the original contours of the courtyard still stand, albeit with a new outline; here, there is a certain tension between new and old, between straight lines and curved. Existing soil has been built into the terrain, to create a hilly landscape covered with new topsoil. It is traversed by two diagonal paths, in oversized standard concrete slabs, that connect the courtyard's different functions.

The new utility building partly consists of the existing glass-covered steel structure, which is enclosed by a newly-built wooden structure. It has been turned inside out, exposing the structural members: its espalier-like appearance is more like a garden pavilion than a utility building. By using this structure as the central motif, the cladding could be done in simple painted spruce plywood sheets. The rhythmic structure brings a sense of cohesion to the building, while also breaking it down into smaller segments. A recess creates a cover in front of the pram room. Insulated parts are covered in external plywood sheets, with an actual espalier reflecting the load-bearing structure in terms of dimension and rhythm. The side facing the courtyard garden is clad in mirrors, mounted directly upon the old steel structure, thus expanding the experience of the green landscape. The mirroring façade is likewise fitted with espalier, referencing the load-bearing structure. These alterations to the structure create variations on the same theme, depending on the viewing angle.

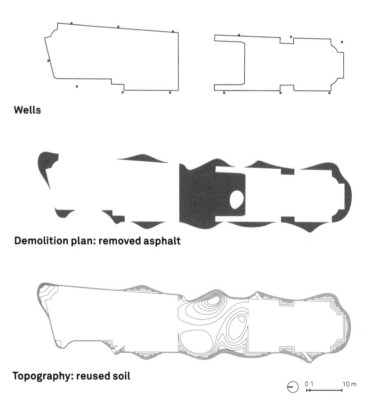

Wells

Demolition plan: removed asphalt

Topography: reused soil

0 1   10 m

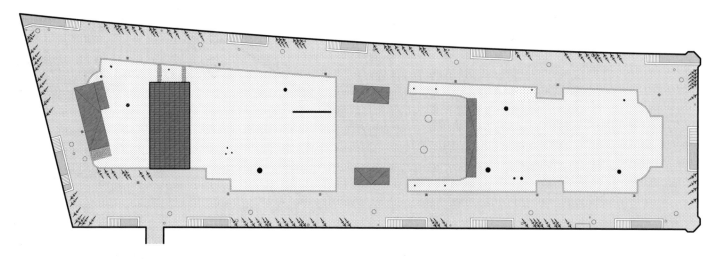

General plan before transformation

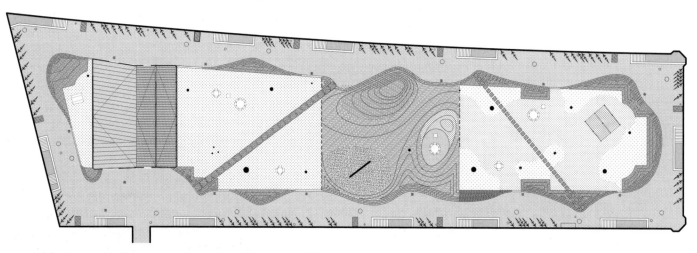

General plan after transformation

0 1   10 m

Transformation of Nørrehus courtyard, Copenhagen

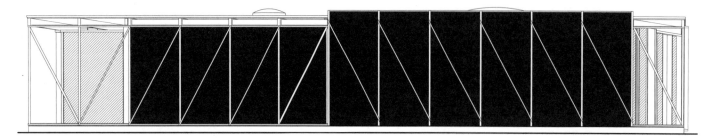

North elevation

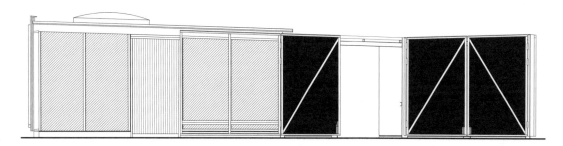

East elevation

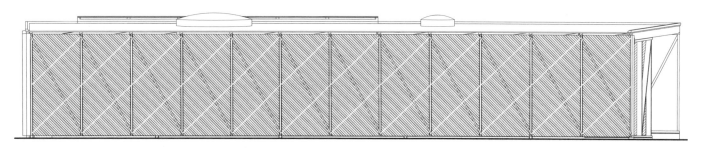

South elevation

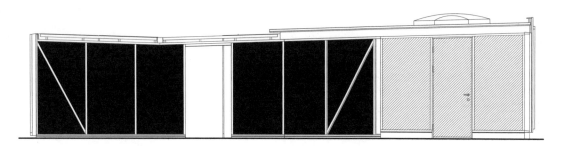

West elevation

Transformation of Nørrehus courtyard, Copenhagen

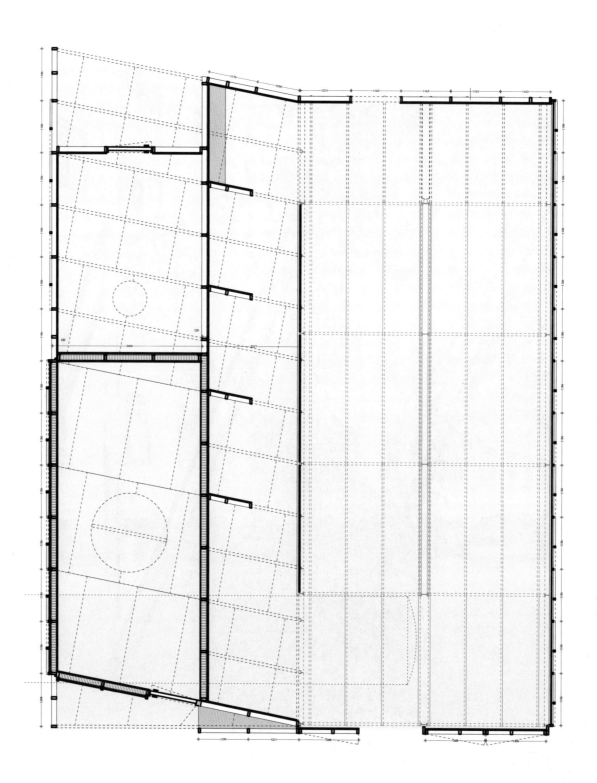

Ground floor plan

0   1   2 m

Transformation of Nørrehus courtyard, Copenhagen

Transformation of three pump stations, Skjern River
2013-15

As a result of the restoration of the Skjern River basin in 2002, a vast and rich natural area has arisen, and it is now an attractive visitor destination. A blueprint for the area's new lease of life has been provided with the rebuilding and extension of three pump stations: they offer exhibition spaces, indoor and outdoor viewpoints to look out over the landscape, rooms for holding events and improved accessibility.

The extensions and the new interior building elements are mainly simple wooden constructions that reiterate the dimensions and rhythm of the original pump stations' concrete relief. This creates a direct link between the old structure and the new, while also adding a new material and a different texture that is pleasing to the touch.

With this detail, the cladding and the main structure become one, reducing the complexity of the building; this is reflected in the budget, as well as the final expression.

Myhrwold & Rasmussen engineered the original pump stations, from 1966, to be unsentimental and raw in their materiality. The vertical relief of the concrete façades reminds us of the ploughed furrows of the surrounding fields and the profiles of the soil that guide the run of the river. By building on this motif, the buildings are more strongly anchored into the surroundings and the history of the site.

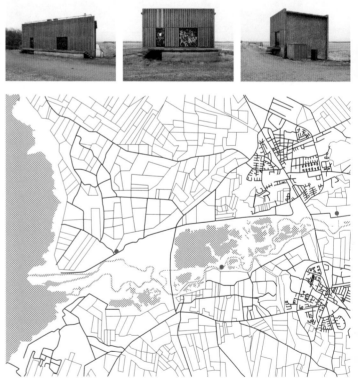

General plan before the restoration of the river basin

General plan after the restoration of the river basin

East pump station

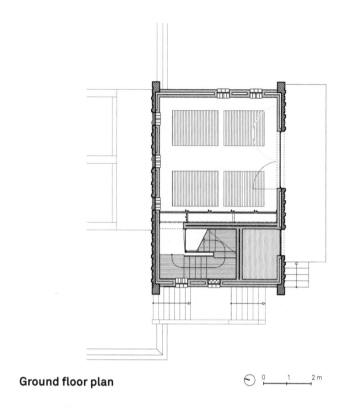

Ground floor plan

0   1   2 m

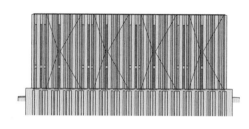

South elevation

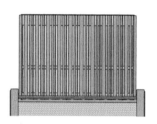

West elevation

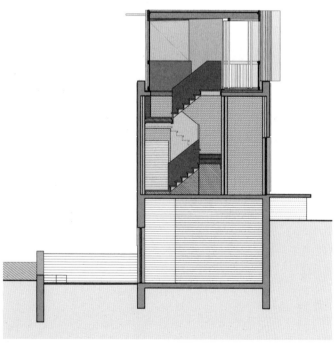

Cross-section

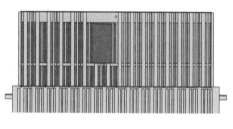

North elevation

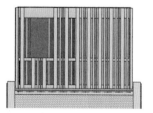

East elevation

Transformation of three pump stations, Skjern River

North pump station

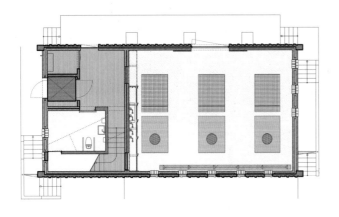

Ground floor plan

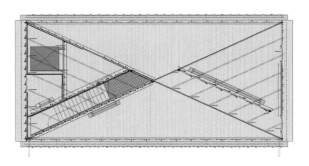

Roof plan

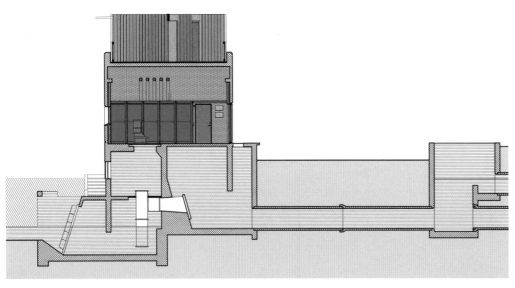

Cross-section

South elevation

East elevation

North elevation

West elevation

Transformation of three pump stations, Skjern River

Transformation of three pump stations, Skjern River

Transformation of three pump stations, Skjern River

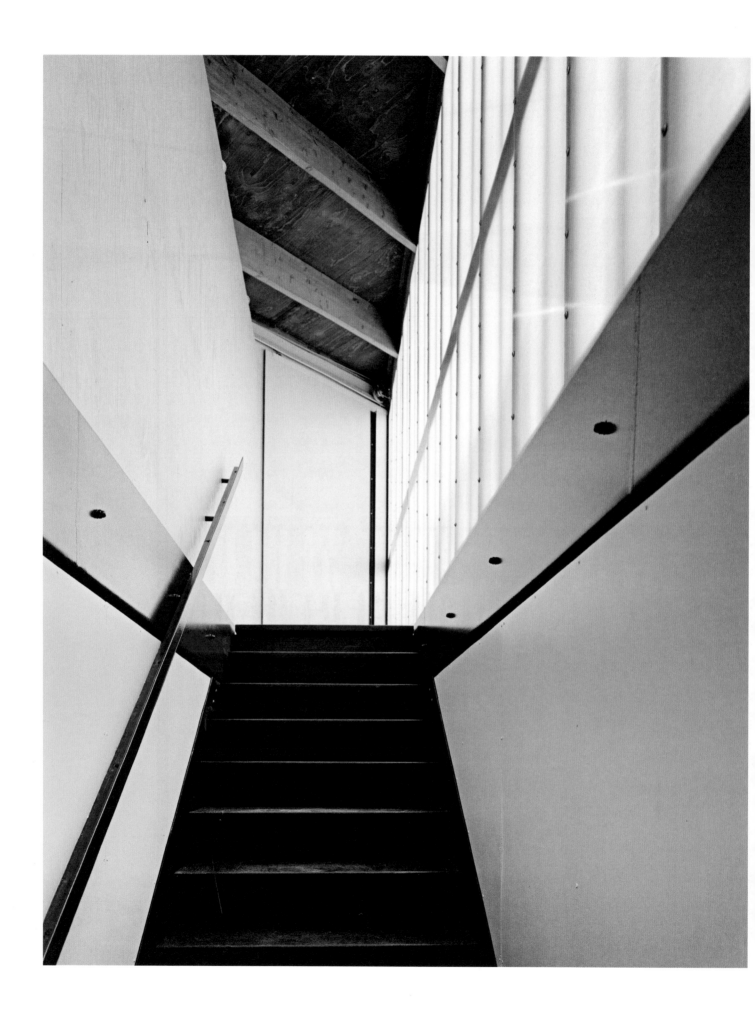

South pump station

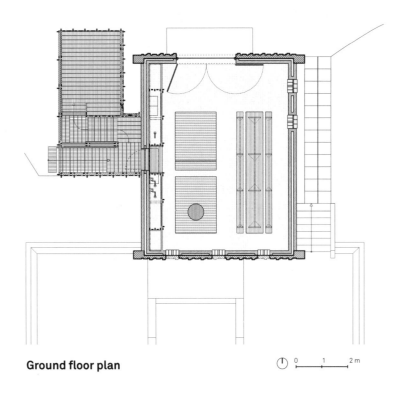

Ground floor plan

0   1   2 m

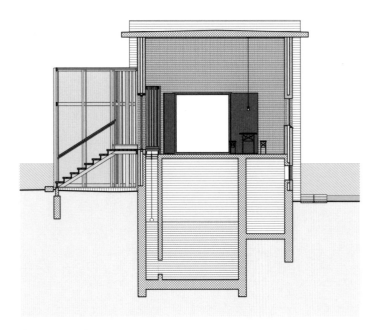

Cross-section

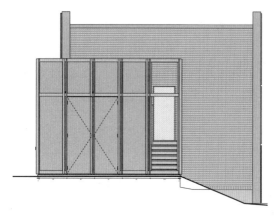

West elevation

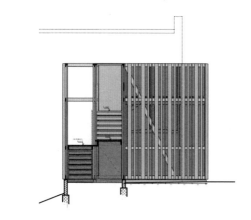

South elevation

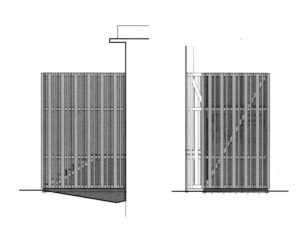

East elevation   **North elevation**

Transformation of three pump stations, Skjern River

Bird sanctuary, Tipperne

2012-17

The bird sanctuary at the tip of the peninsula in the southern part of Ringkøbing Fjord is, with its unique nature, an important stopping-off point for migratory birds, and it is home to Europe's oldest continuous bird counts. Previously, public access to the area was very limited, but the area has now been opened to visitors following the creation of new facilities. They are simple instrument-like additions to the landscape: a bird hide, watchtower, workshop, walking routes and the conversion of the Tipper House research station. The new structures are imagined as freestanding objects in the landscape, each with distinctive characteristics and subtle mutual relationships with one another and their surroundings.

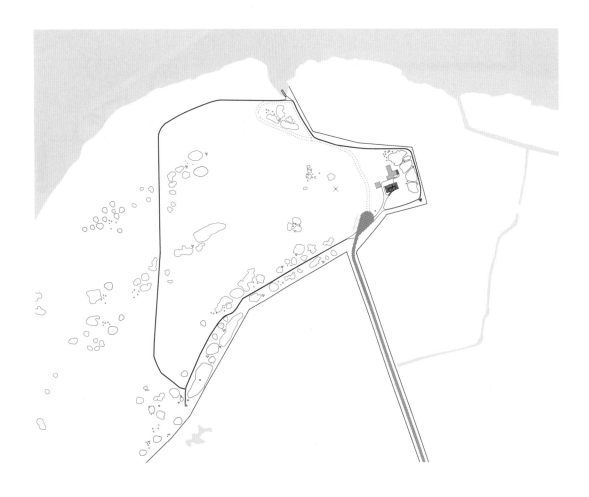

Tower

The birdwatching tower was developed through the synthesis of the open, flat wetland geography, with its dense moisture in the air, and the techniques of a local factory that specialises in the production of masts in solid, cylindrical iron bars. The platform provides an elevated framing of the landscape, a space which can be either closed (to offer a secluded spot for bird counters) or opened up to the view. The structural system is designed as a jettying frame that expands in width as it rises, allowing a small footprint to widen incrementally, supporting a larger platform above. Horizontal elements of galvanised iron plates have been bolted and welded together, whilst vertical and diagonal galvanised cylindrical iron bars span between these plates. 50 mm and 65 mm diameter columns and diagonals take compression forces, whilst 22 mm diameter cylindrical iron bars, which form both the balustrade and handrails, transfer tensile forces. All individual elements, including handrails, stairs, landings and balustrades, form part of the tower's overall structural system.

Ground preparation

Bird sanctuary, Tipperne

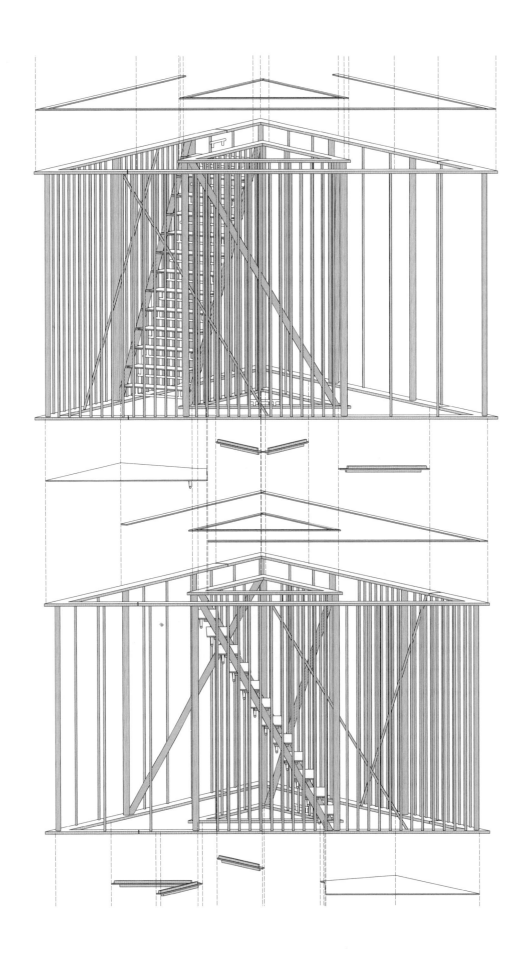

Bird sanctuary, Tipperne

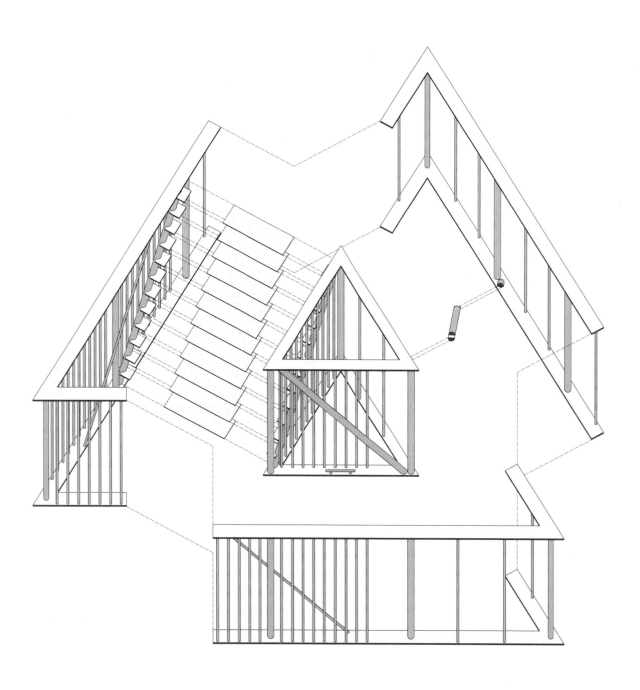

58

Bird sanctuary, Tipperne

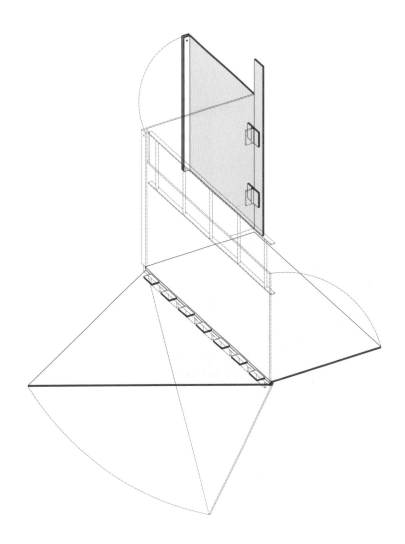

Bird sanctuary, Tipperne

Bird hide

The bird hide is a triangular steel structure which acts as a stop-off point along a walking trail. Visitors can enter a raised hidden platform, from which wildlife can be seen up-close through a narrow slot opening. The structure is assembled using 6 mm plates of Corten steel, with edge reinforcements that simultaneously function as assembly profiles and gutters whilst connecting the structure into the terrain.

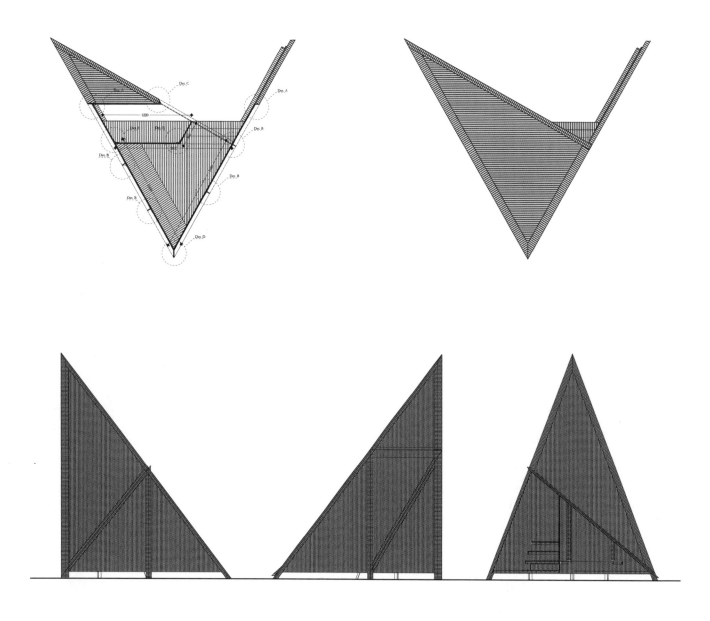

Bird sanctuary, Tipperne

Workshop

The workshop building refers to a small local settlement of improvised hunting huts. It is built as a simple timber frame structure, stiffened and sealed by 3 mm aluminium plates on the inside. The exterior is painted in contrast to the untreated aluminium, revealed internally. Light penetrates the structure through translucent fibreglass boards.

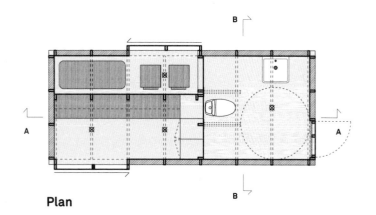

Plan

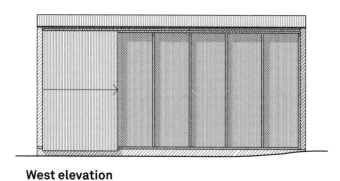

West elevation

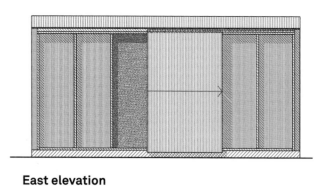

East elevation

Section AA

Section BB

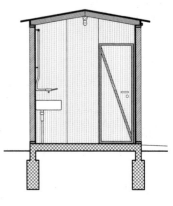

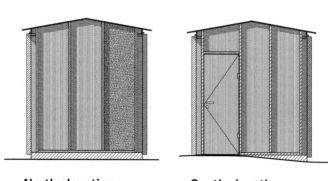

North elevation   **South elevation**

Bird sanctuary, Tipperne

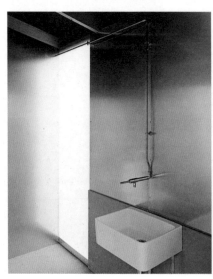

Research station

The existing Tipper House has been transformed into a visitor centre and research station. On the ground floor, the building now hosts exhibitions, a multipurpose room, dining room and kitchen; there is now a library with a workspace on the first floor, and alcove sleeping areas in the gables. In order to retain the quality and character of the existing building, the renovation was carried out via a number of subtle interventions. A new external ramp is the only alteration visible from the exterior; inside, new beams and columns replace and reinforce the load-bearing walls, and a bespoke table and benches feature in the communal areas. Meanwhile, red pipes, radiators and wind gauges draw attention to the research function of the building. The built-in OSB furniture, among other things, forms a new archive for bird counts which has a textural quality reminiscent of the plants in the landscape and the thatch of the roof.

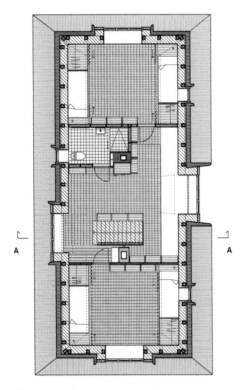

First floor

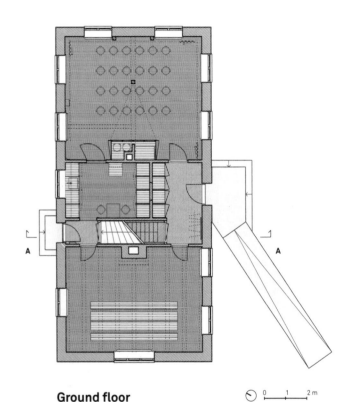

Ground floor

0 1 2 m

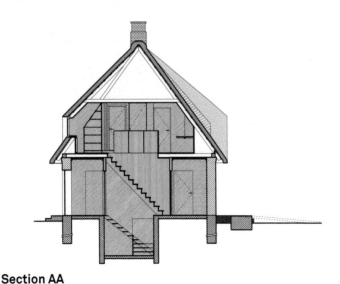

Section AA

Bird sanctuary, Tipperne

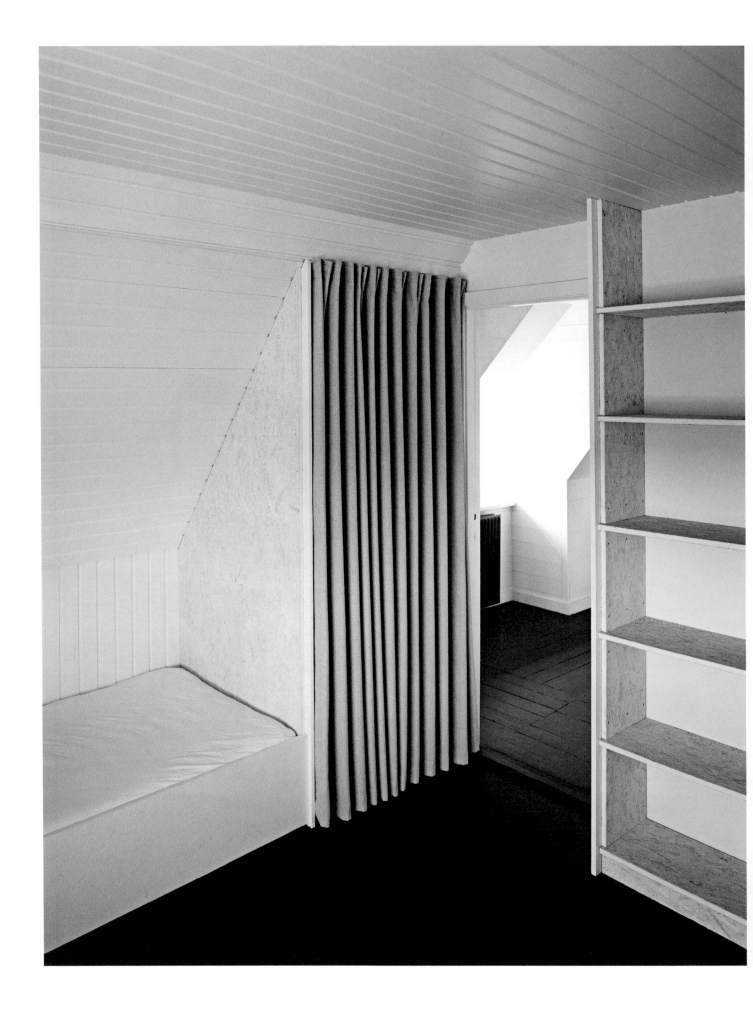

Bird sanctuary, Tipperne

Bakkedraget, Denmark

2015-18

This project is a reinterpretation of a historic cottage and shed. The cottage is located within a protected landscape alongside historic vacation homes, carefully nestled amid slopes of overgrown moraine and sand dunes that rise from the surrounding flatlands. The aim of the reconstruction was to recreate the quality and atmosphere of being in the old cottage before it was abandoned, and before the ensuing timber infestation made its rebuilding inevitable.

The building dates back to 1905: at first, it was two detached log houses, later merged by the addition of a kitchen. It was gradually transformed over time, including architect Ivar Bentsen's addition of a stove and chimney, as well as the introduction of a new shed.

The structure is rebuilt as a lightweight timber frame construction, insulated with paper- and wood fibers, allowing the exterior to retain the protected expression of the old cottage. The new interior interprets the memories and accumulated features for contemporary conditions, informed by the modern structure, and expressed through partially painted wooden surfaces, peculiar alcoves and niches.

The exterior walls are internally clad in wide horizontal boards, referring to the formerly exposed logs. The walls separating rooms are clad in thinner vertical boards. Pressure-resistant wood fiber insulation in the roof enables the rafters to remain exposed. The original disposition of the rooms has been altered slightly; walls separating shared spaces have been removed, though the separation they created can still be traced through material changes. A tiled grid is laid out in the hallway, kitchen and bathroom, shifting in colour between the spaces. Wooden walls are left untreated or otherwise painted in colours drawn from the old interior. Niches and alcoves are recreated by leaving wooden surfaces unpainted.

These strategies allow the rooms and the overall layout to be continuous yet self-contained, introducing a density of personal unconventional spaces. The original cottages' complexity is reinterpreted as a clearly defined patchwork of shifting materials and colours, visible from one room to the next, thereby creating a contemporary space that pragmatically reinterprets the past.

Cottage

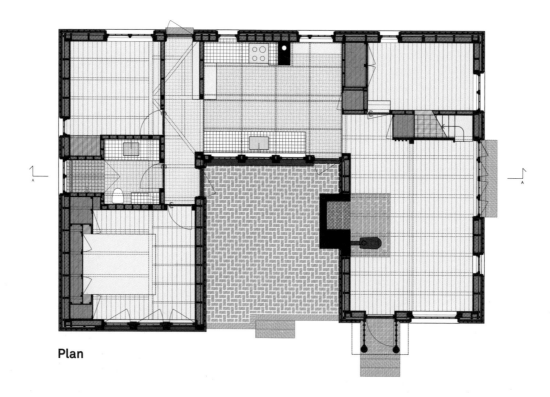

Plan

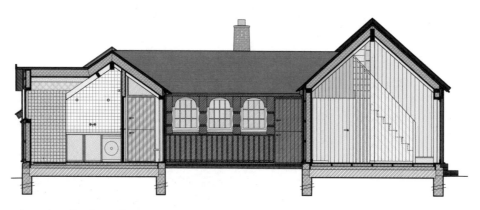

Longitudinal section

Shed

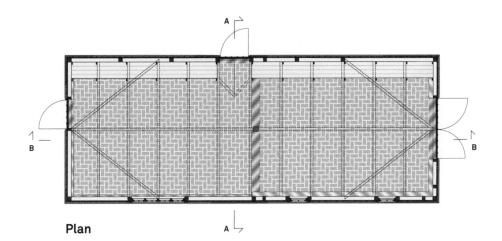

Plan

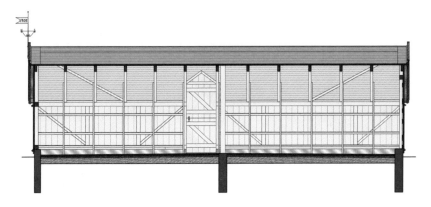

Section BB

Section AA

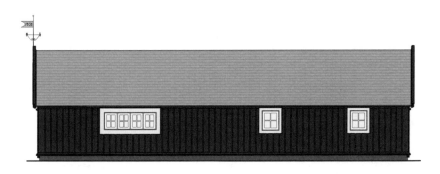

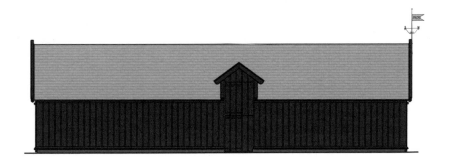

Temporary pavilion, Sydney

2018

To mark the 100th anniversary of Jørn Utzon's birth, and the Sydney Opera House's 45th anniversary, Johansen Skovsted Arkitekter was commissioned to design a temporary pavilion based on Utzon's architectural motifs.

The pavilion is a processed mock-up of a building fragment that never existed, namely one of the plywood beams that, when put together, would make up the ceilings of Utzon's unrealised auditoriums. The beam is placed resting on its side in front of the Opera House (where building parts were stored during the construction period) and processed in form, dimension and construction. Utzon's unrealised design is made accessible as a pavilion. When placed in another context, a new spatial experience occurs, detached from the original intentions.

The pavilion is an elongated sequence of crescent rooms. Its placement creates distinct spaces towards the podium's reddish uniformity, and a closed-off space towards the water-scape. By removing selected sheets, the visitors are invited inside to experience how the pavilion alternatively closes and, through light frames, opens up views of the surroundings.

Originally, the beam was to be constructed in up to 15-metre-long plywood sheets, enabling it to span long intervals. Its new function, and placement on its side, enables a construction in two layers of load-bearing standard-size plywood sheets. The bolts, that hold stiffening blocks between the two layers, form a dotted pattern. Along with the dark blue interior, they create a deep, subdued atmosphere in the bright Sydney light.

In the end, the funding did not come through. The mock-up of an unrealised building fragment was, once again, unrealised.

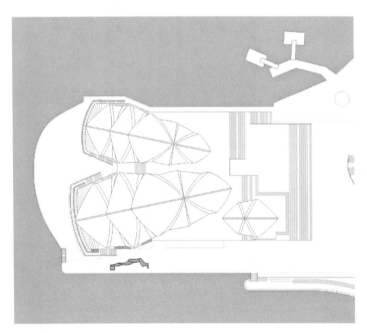

Site plan

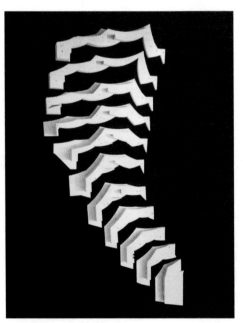

Jørn Utzon, model, beams layout
© Utzon Archive / Utzon Centre

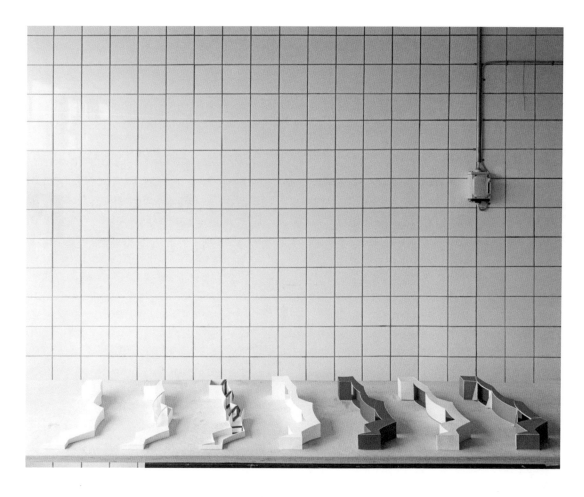

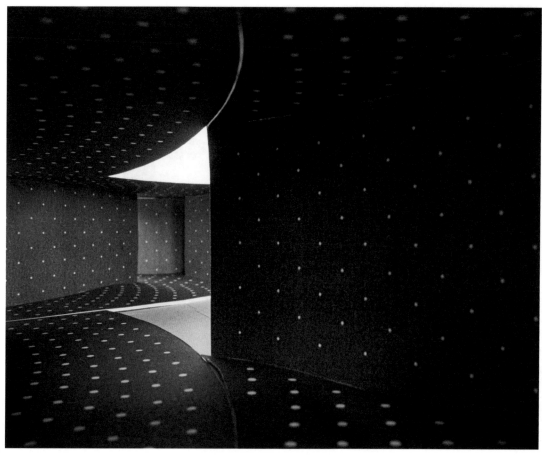

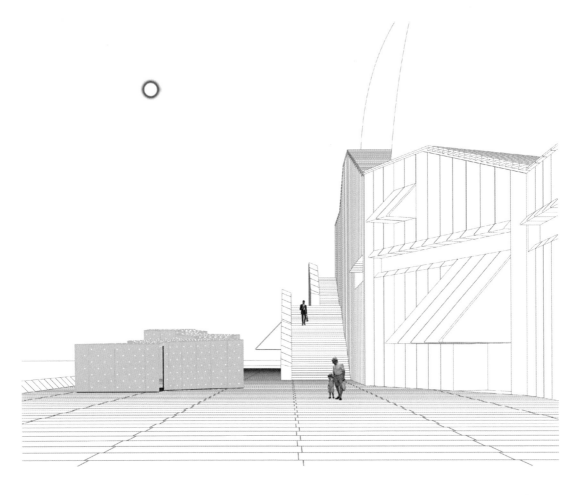

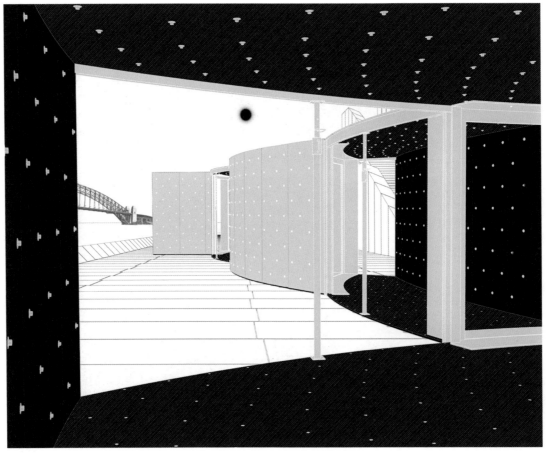

86

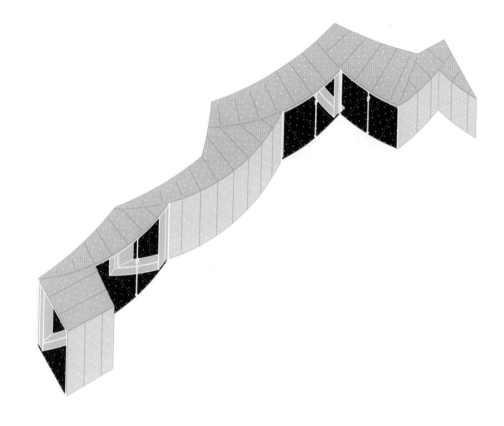

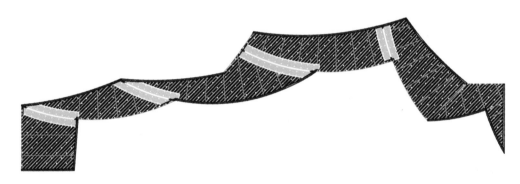

Plan

Elevation

Temporary pavilion, Sydney

CODAN, Køge

2017-23

Office and warehouse

This project is located between the scenic shape of the Køge Bay Highway and the circular infrastructure of Køge University Hospital. It houses the Danish headquarters of the pharmaceutical company CODAN, and has office facilities for the company's ownership group, the associated secretariat and the Danish distribution department. Additionally, the building contains a warehouse with medical devices, for distribution to Danish hospitals.

The building is structured as a series of office wings that articulate the internal structure of the company. They envelop the tall warehouse building and nestle into the terrain with slight shifts in level that follow the curvature of the landscape. All of the office spaces, as well as the warehouse packing areas, are oriented towards the meadow on the southern side of the building, which becomes a unifying landscape space, concluding in a courtyard. In a depression on the meadow, a local rainwater drainage for the facility's rooftop water is placed and shaped as a natural wetland.

The internal flow of the building is arranged like a journey, with generous communal spaces and passageways that create interactions between bright, high-ceilinged rooms and more intimate, secluded passages and niches. In this way, the meeting rooms, offices, warehouses and packing areas are connected to the central communal dining area where employees from all sections of the building come together. The resulting environment allows for both deep concentration and confidentiality, and for a rich social and professional community.

The building complex is constructed using prefabricated concrete elements which, due to their thermal mass, mitigate fluctuations in temperature; in doing so, the building complies with the rigorous standards for temperature stability with regards to storing pharmaceuticals. The moulded façade panels are designed with a relief that shifts the façade plane and creates a rhythm that manages to connect the open offices with the large, enclosed warehouse.

CODAN, Køge

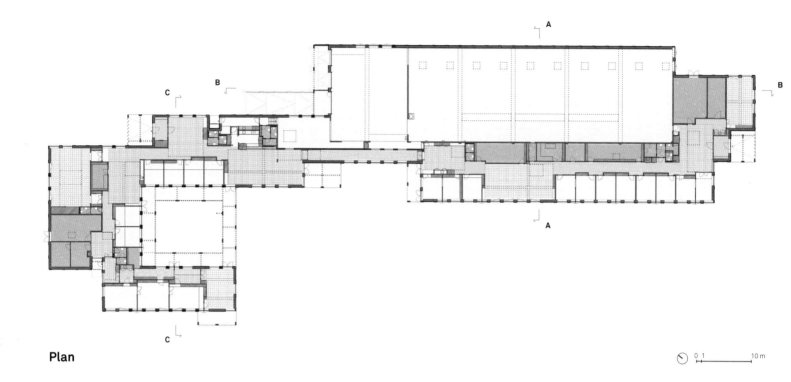

Plan

East elevation

West elevation

South elevation

North elevation

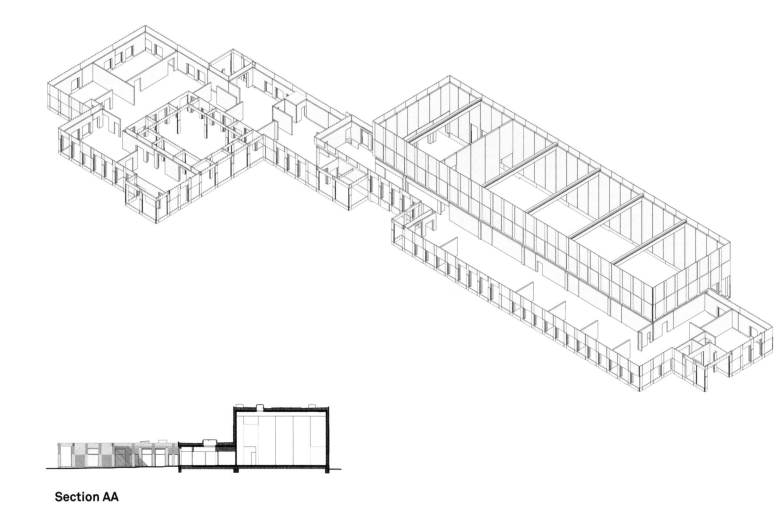

Section AA

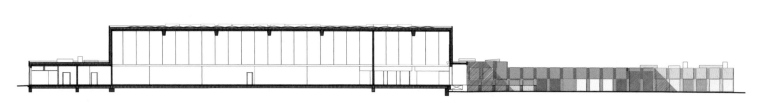

Section BB

Section CC

CODAN, Køge

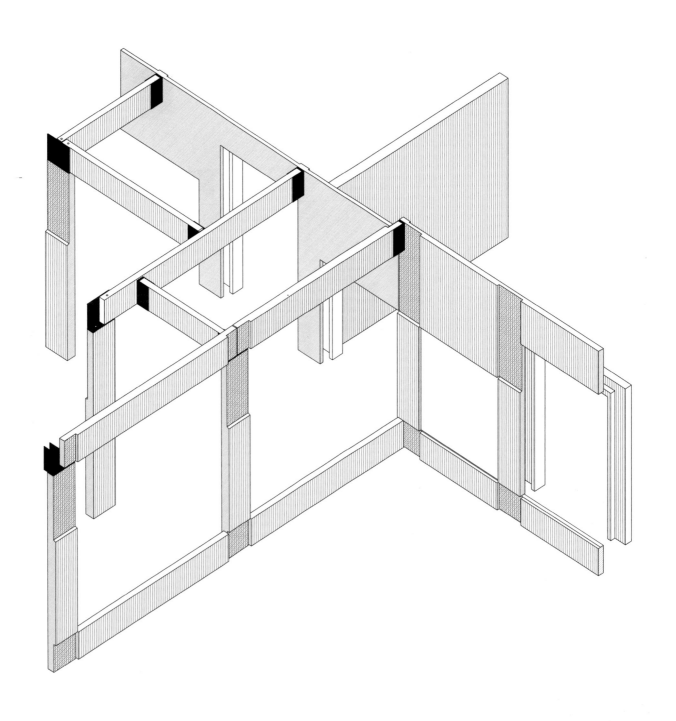

CODAN, Køge

CODAN, Køge

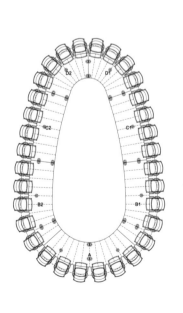

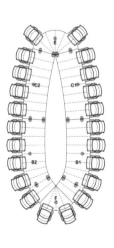

CODAN, Køge

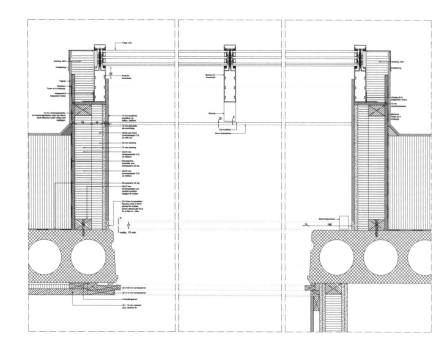

CODAN, Køge

Utility buildings

As part of the building complex, two utility buildings have been erected. The smaller building contains a storage room for machinery and other equipment, while the larger building features a container yard, a room for waste and recycling, storage, and a covered space for bicycle parking.

The utility buildings are constructed as prefabricated, demountable steel structures made of bent and bolted galvanised and painted plates, forming wall- and roof modules. These elements serve as the structure's load-bearing, bracing, and enclosing parts. They interact with the colours and rhythm of the large concrete element building, simultaneously creating contrast and coherence.

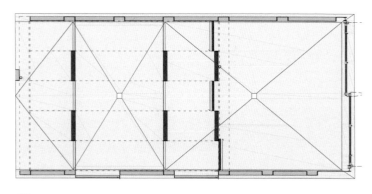

Plan

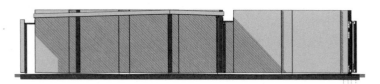

Longitudinal section

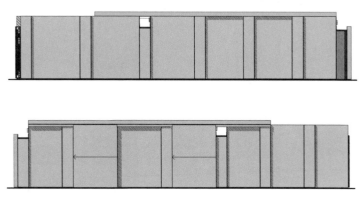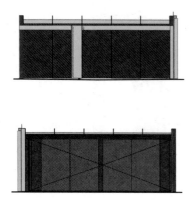

Elevations

CODAN, Køge

Alternative Histories exhibition, London
2019

For the exhibition *Alternative Histories*, initiated by Drawing Matter and The Architecture Foundation, we were asked to imagine an alternative future for a historical architectural drawing, to be presented in the form of a model. We were assigned the drawing *Untitled 1226* (1980-99) by Peter Märkli.

The result is a model that elaborates upon certain ideas suggested in the drawing. The model's proportions and dimensions are directly transferred from the drawing, if read as an elevation. In the drawing, the layered squares and lines create depth, generating a foreground and background; subsequently, in the model, these elements become openings and views. The model is not to be read as a finished proposition, but rather as a concentrated study of the proportions and spatial transitions originating from Peter Märkli's drawing.

The model is constructed in 754 white aerated concrete blocks. All blocks are cut by hand to the dimensions 15 × 20 × 30 mm, and are then joined with adhesive. The interior walls intertwine into each other's bonds for strength and stability, but they overlap with the outer walls at just two points per wall, to prevent the wall from being weakened by a vertical bonding. The merge between the inner and outer walls creates a displacement of the vertical line in the façade, and thus breaks up the repetitive block structure. The inner openings are placed systematically in each wall section; the exterior openings, meanwhile, are shaped according to the proportions of the drawing, and are arranged strategically to frame certain views in the enclosed upper part.

The aerated concrete blocks represent a readable scale and refer to a particular building technique, but the tectonics of the model creates an abstraction in scale. The model appears both in its own right as an object at 1:1, and as a representation in 1:20. At 1:1, the construction does not require any additional structural elements for creating openings and cantilevers: it is held up by the fixed bricks. This results in a stable structure, simultaneously stacked and hanging.

Due to its heavy top and light bottom, the model was built upside down. This technique generates a duality, whereby the model can be perceived either way round. Different qualities emerge depending on how the object is staged, evoking a new dialogue around the model and its relation to Märkli's initial drawing.

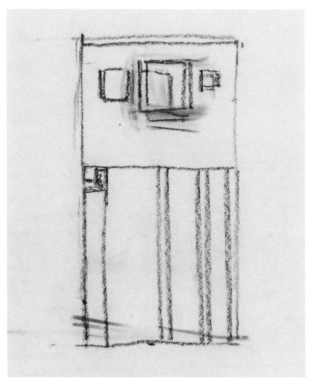

Peter Märkli, *Untitled 1226*, 1980-99
Drawing Matter Collection; © Peter Märkli

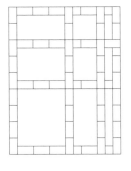 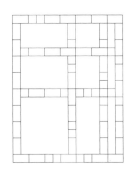  

  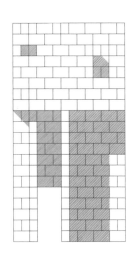 

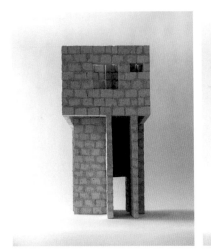 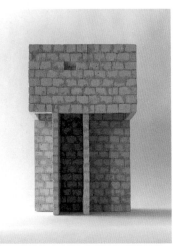  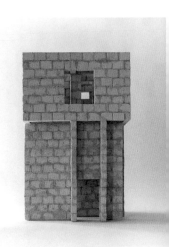

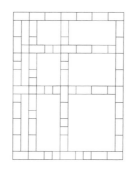
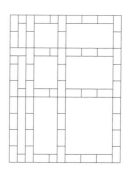

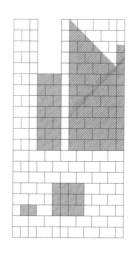

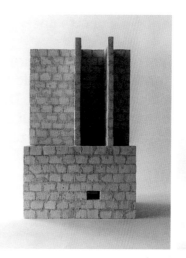
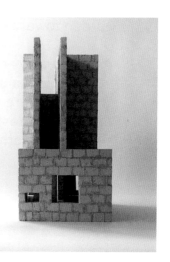

Alternative Histories exhibition, London

Shelving, Marienborg

2017-19

Marienborg is a listed building from 1745, located north of Copenhagen in a former Baroque garden overlooking Lyngby Lake. Marienborg serves as the official residence for Denmark's prime minister, and is frequently used for governmental conferences, meetings and other official purposes. Marienborg's front-of-house has undergone an interior renovation by Mathias and Nikolaj Menze, with site-specific contributions from various Danish contemporary designers, architects and artists.

As part of the renovation, Johansen Skovsted Arkitekter were invited to make two specialised pieces of furniture for Marienborg's library and for a small sitting room above. The furniture is built as a simple assemblage of standard brass profiles, functioning as an open shelving rack in the library and a sideboard in the sitting room. By combining precious materials and refined craftsmanship, the furniture creates a domestic atmosphere, suitable for confidential conversations and important decisions. The two pieces take up a central location on the first and second floors of the building, and they appear as an extension of each other; they complete the axis that runs from Lyngby Lake and through the garden towards Marienborg's centre line.

An exploration of proportions and structural stability is the basis for the system in which the shelves are dimensioned and divided. Their upward progression enhances the relation between the overlying rooms, while the horizontal offset and subtle shear of their profiles manages to create a perspectival depth between the front and back of the structure. The interplay between squares and rectangles provides a certain order and suggests ways in which the addition of books and objects can create a variation in expression and use.

The customised brass shelving is produced by local blacksmith Emil Nielsen, and is assembled as a simple construction made of 15 × 15 mm standard brass profiles for the main structure and 2 mm brass plates for the shelves and stiffening element. The vertical and horizontal profiles are fixed in three-point screw joints and mounted to the rear wall by anchored points for cross-stabilisation. All screws are hidden, contributing to a light structure. The brass surface has been given only a light sanding, and will patinate through usage, over time.

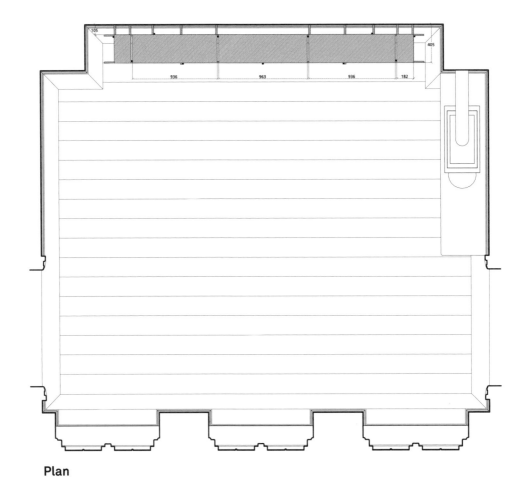

Plan

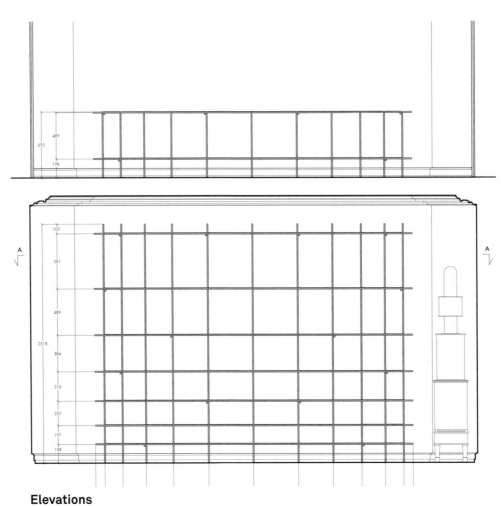

Elevations

Shelving, Marienborg

Shelving, Marienborg

Laveskov, Sletten

2018-23

Located by the Øresund coast near Sletten Harbour, this house sits in a diverse residential neighbourhood of older villas, newer catalogue houses and fishing huts. Numerous buildings feature yellow stone, while others have yellow-and-white painted plastered exteriors. Laveskov's long roof serves to mirror the existing pitched roof of Slettenhus. These two buildings, perpendicular to the coast, create a framing of the public beach park. A narrow, projecting façade, facing the Gl. Strandvej road, makes a discreet impression from the street.

The owners — a couple whose way of life is closely connected with nature and the sea — wanted a home that would reflect and complement their lifestyle. The long, stepped building volume forms a layout of staggered rooms, diagonally interconnected at the corners. These connections create views of the landscape and the sea from all main rooms, and a non-hierarchical interweaving of spaces, both inside and out. In the deep passages between the rooms, the wooden surfaces are left unpainted to create a clear spatial delineation.

Around the building, smaller auxiliary structures contain a garden shed, a workshop and a sauna. An entrance courtyard, a morning terrace with an outdoor kitchen, a covered evening terrace and a framed herb garden are formed between these structures and the main building, where they are sheltered from the sometimes-harsh weather of Øresund. These outdoor spaces are integrated with the building's interior spaces, due to the equality of the overall spatial structure.

The framed herb garden by the road stands as a cultivated, planted area. The rest of the landscape around the building is low-maintenance and "natural" in appearance, extending the native plants and grasses of the beach and windbreak.

The exterior walls of the house are stabilised by tensioned steel columns. The walls are constructed using insulated lightweight blocks clad with yellow brick shells, which have been mounted without bond in a vertical direction, using visible mortar joints. Along the exterior spaces of the house, the blocks are painted white to create a uniformity with the white spaces indoors.

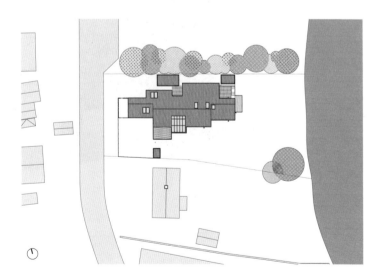

Laveskov, Sletten

North elevation

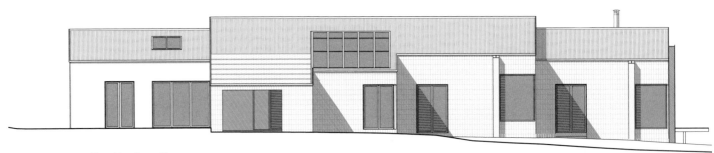

South elevation

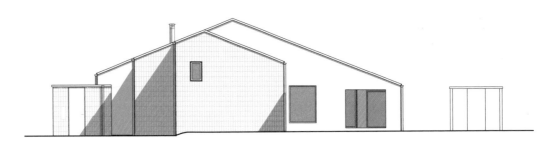

West elevation

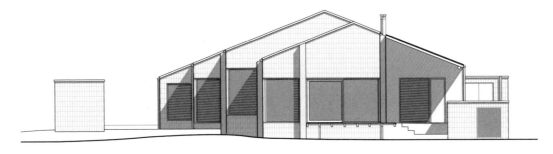

East elevation

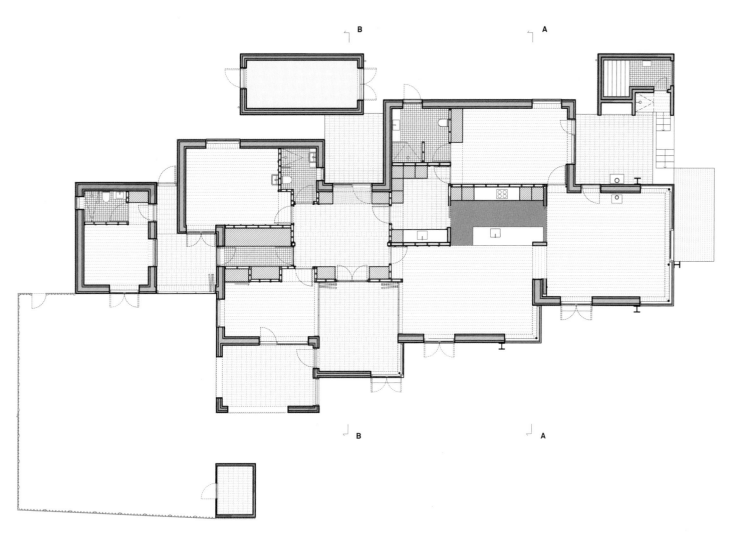

Ground floor

0 1 2 m

Laveskov, Sletten

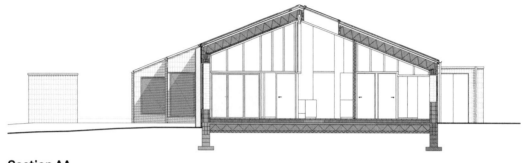

Section AA

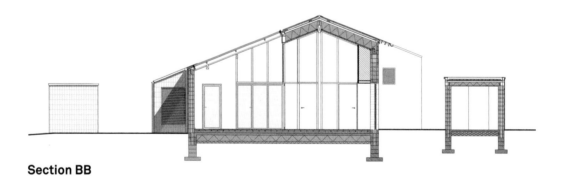

Section BB

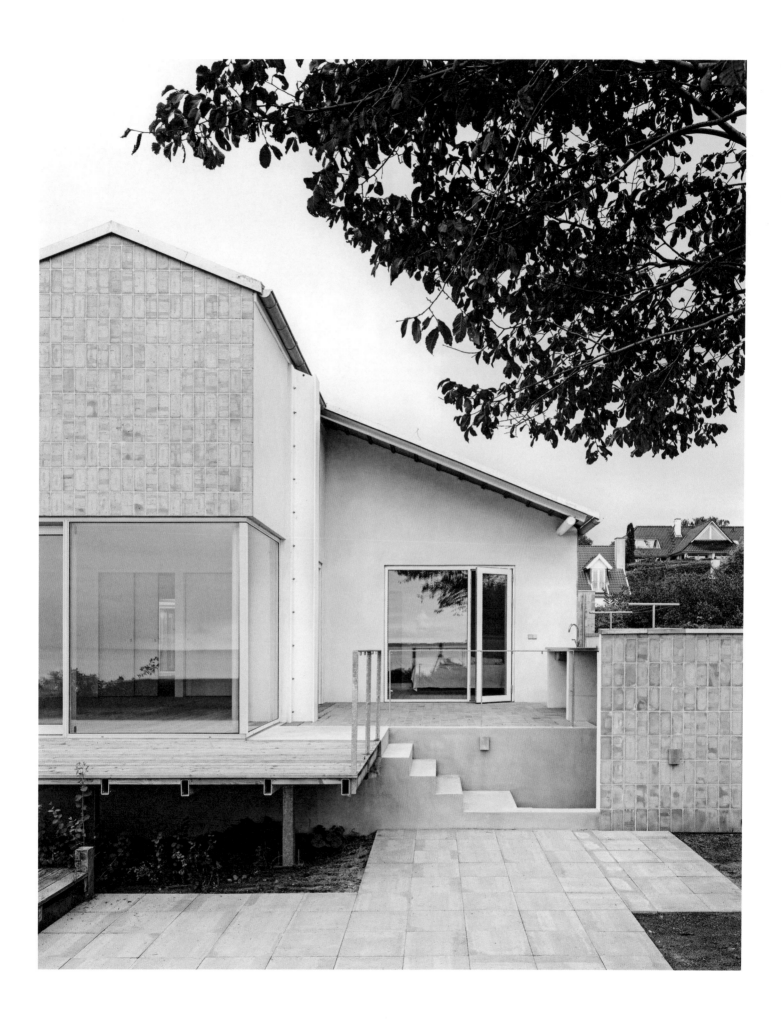

1 Ridge beam: 140 × 366 mm
2 Ridge vent
3 Roof construction: zinc roof plate: sinus 18/76 mm
  Pine boarding: 25 × 115 mm
  Pine battens
  Rockwool insulation: 380 mm
  Vapour retarding layer
  Counterbattens: two layers of 22 × 100 mm battens
  Pine ceiling boards: 19 × 125 mm, white lacquered
4 Top plate: 45 × 180 mm
5 Wall construction
  Brick shells: 25 mm
  Adhesive mortar: 10 mm
  Finja Exact lightweight concrete block: 400 mm
6 Rigid insulation
7 Floor construction
  Floorboards: pine 250 × 35 mm
  Underlayment
  Heat emission plate: 22 mm
  Lath
  Floor joists
  Insulation between joists
  Concrete floor slab
  Insulation
  Radon barrier
8 Stone water drain

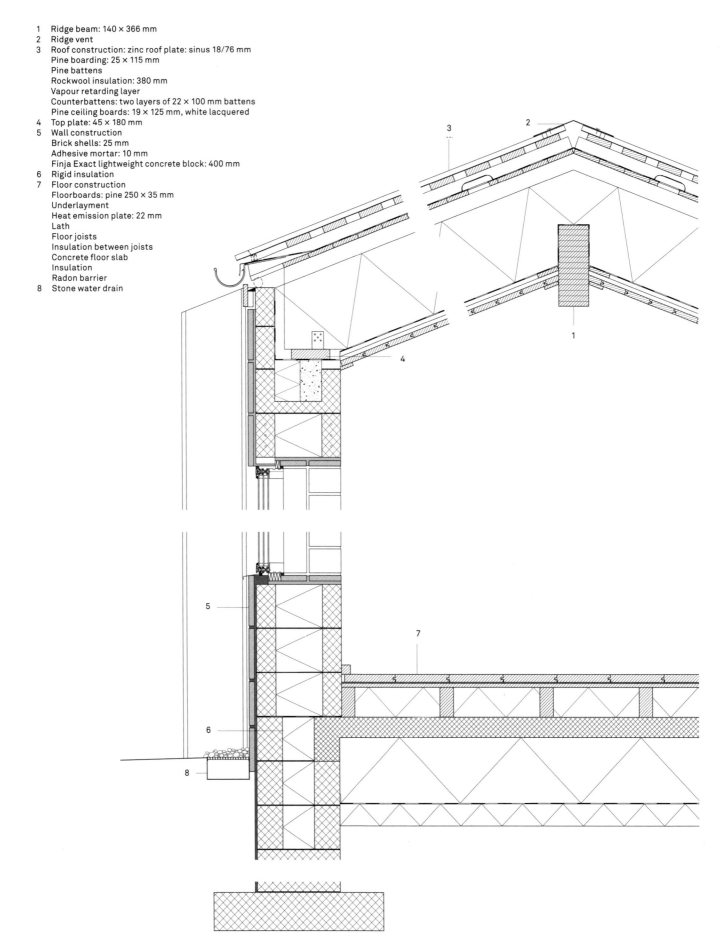

Laveskov, Sletten

Transformation of water tower, Groenendijk

2021-

This project is a winning competition entry for the conversion of a functioning post-war water tower from 1969, located in Groenendijk, near the Flemish coast. The brief was to make the tower accessible to the public, and enable visitors to experience the panoramic views of the coastal region.

The proposal adds two new elements to the iconic silhouette of the existing water tower, creating a vertical ensemble consisting of an elevator tower and a stairway winding upwards between the two towers. The result is an ensemble of elements, old and new, which all contribute to the spatial and structural logic.

In the landscape, at the entrance to the site, visitors are greeted by a small utility pavilion, marking the start of the route through the pine forest towards the foot of the ascending stairway. The experience of traversing the stairs is like that of a meandering mountain path, with plateaus along the way offering new views of the coastal area and new spaces between existing

and added structures in the otherwise flat landscape of the region. At the summit, the pavilion on top of the water tower is transformed into a multifunctional "cloud chamber", housing a café and spaces for meetings, educational events and social gatherings.

The elevator tower and stair are made in metallised steel, contrasting with the concrete tower. Their detailing, however, clearly celebrates the character of the existing structure, with vertical lines and the fan-shape motif visible from below. The stairs are executed in thin steel plates that are welded to and cantilever from the main beam which, through its design and connections to the two towers, withstands all torsional and tensile forces, thus forming a coherent structural whole.

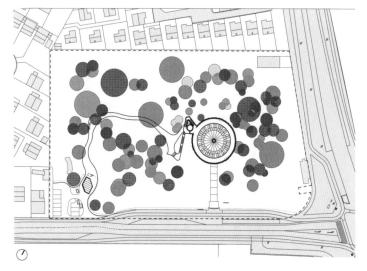

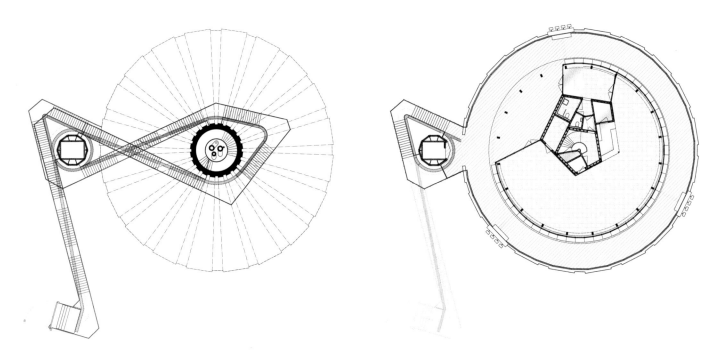

Plan: stairway

Plan: cloud chamber

Credits

Transformation of Nørrehus courtyard

Location Nørrebro (Copenhagen), Denmark
Architects Johansen Skovsted Arkitekter
Design and construction years 2014 (landscape), 2014-16 (building)
Collaborator Sidse Hald (first phase)
Client Ejerforeningen Nørrehus
Engineer Okholm ApS
Contractors Sven Bech A/S and Kjell Pedersen A/S
Photographs Rasmus Norlander and Johansen Skovsted Arkitekter

Transformation of three pump stations

Location Skjern River, West Jutland, Denmark
Architects Johansen Skovsted Arkitekter
Design and construction years 2013-15
Collaborator Bertelsen & Scheving Arkitekter
Client Ringkøbing-Skjern Kommune; financially supported by Realdania - Stedet Tæller and LAG-Ringkøbing-Skjern
Engineer Ingeniørgruppen Vestjylland ApS
Contractor Hansen & Larsen A/S
Photographs Rasmus Norlander

Bird sanctuary

Location Tipperne, Ringkøbing Fjord, Denmark
Architects Johansen Skovsted Arkitekter
Design and construction years 2012-17
Collaborator Bertelsen & Scheving Arkitekter
Client The Danish Nature Agency; financially supported by Realdania - Stedet Tæller
Engineer Ingeniørgruppen Vestjylland ApS
Engineer tower NordBase Engineering ApS
Contractors Bendt K Jensen A/S and Carl C A/S (tower and bird hide)
Photographs Rasmus Norlander, Rasmus Hjortshøj and Johansen Skovsted Arkitekter

Bakkedraget

Location Denmark
Architects Johansen Skovsted Arkitekter and LASC
Design and construction years 2015-18
Engineer Ingeniørgruppen Vestjylland
Photographs Laura Stamer

Temporary pavilion

Location Western Boardwalk, Sydney, Australia
Architects Johansen Skovsted Arkitekter
Design and construction year 2018
Client Utzon Center; financially supported by The Danish Arts Foundation

CODAN

Location Køge, Denmark
Architects Johansen Skovsted Arkitekter
Design and construction years 2017-23
Client CODAN Companies ApS
Landscape architect Marianne Levinsen Landskab
Engineer Strunge Jensen A/S
Contractors MT Højgaard (lead contractor), Ambercon (concrete elements), Malmos (landscape), Kecon (steel), Raaschou Inventar (build-in furniture)
Photographs Rasmus Norlander

Alternative Histories exhibition

Location London, UK
Design and construction year 2019
Architects Johansen Skovsted Arkitekter
Curator Marius Grootveld, Veldwerk

Photographs Johansen Skovsted Arkitekter

Shelving

Location Marienborg, North Zealand, Denmark
Architects Johansen Skovsted Arkitekter
Design and construction years 2017-19
Client The Prime Minister's Office
Estate holder Agency for Culture and Palaces
Blacksmith Emil Nielsen Smedeværksted A/S
Photographs Laura Stamer

Laveskov

Location Sletten, Denmark
Architects Johansen Skovsted Arkitekter and LASC
Design and construction year 2018-23
Engineer Ingeniørgruppen Vestjylland ApS
Photographs Hampus Berndtson

Transformation of water tower

Location Groenendijk, Oostduinkerke, Belgium
Architects Johansen Skovsted Arkitekter and Veldhuis architectuur
Design and construction years 2021-
Collaborator Veldhuis Architectuur
Client IWVA/Aquaduin
Structural engineer Servais Engineering Architectural
Special techniques Studieburo George
Landscape architects Bureau Cnockaert

NEXUS

On Ole Meyer
Six short photo-essays

Søren Johansen, Sebastian Skovsted

The carpenter, architect and photographer Ole Meyer is, at least internationally, one of the lesser-known figures of mid-century Danish architecture. The subjects of his photography, as well as his ability to both observe and establish a connection between observation and design, have been a source of inspiration to us ever since we first came across his work.

Meyer was born in 1929, and he completed his architecture studies at the Royal Academy in Copenhagen in 1955. This was a time of profound transition: the post-war industrialisation of the building sector was picking up pace, and would soon become dominant in the early sixties.

Meyer referred to himself as being of the "functional tradition", a phrase coined by Kay Fisker, who was a frequent lecturer at the Academy during Meyer's student days. It was believed that this architecture — without stylistic genealogy or "pedigree", but derived from its purpose and a material culture — would have longevity due to its universal nature.

During the 1950s and thereafter, Meyer documented local, anonymous utility structures like greenhouses, barns and brickworks. These photographs celebrate the unadorned structures of early industrialisation, evoking a

Ole Meyer (photographer), timber drying in Roskilde, Denmark, 1950
© Ole Meyer / Jens Bertelsen

Ole Meyer (architect and photographer), his parents summer house in Røsnæs, Denmark, 1963
© Ole Meyer / Jens Bertelsen

beauty they did not claim for themselves. In this photographic work, there is a search for structural and spatial qualities, stemming from the necessary, the pragmatic, the constructed; this work was explicitly intended to be a source of inspiration for himself, as well as architects in general. As with his gaze through the camera, his architectural perspective was curated: he would selectively frame and transplant certain aspects of his observations into his work as an architect. On the potential of his observations from brickworks, Meyer stated:

> The proportions, material frugality, variation, etc., were an inspiration that could well be transferred as a collective effort towards lightness and restrained material consumption.[1]

Today, architects are again faced with a time of fundamental change in society and more specifically the building industry, as major recalibrations are needed to avoid global environmental collapse. We therefore believe that Meyer and his generation have a renewed relevance in this time, given his efforts to frame his observations in a way that treated obsolete structures with dignity and appreciation. Furthermore, Meyer partook in a search for an architecture that was based on an intimate understanding of the specifics of a given physical environment and material culture, whereby spaces and structures would be made with the essential materials needed to provide a framework for daily life.

The following pages are dedicated to six short photo-essays that offer some insight into our endeavours to create connections between observations of landscapes, places, structures, construction processes and manufacturing methods, and the choices that went into two of the projects presented in this publication. This is part of a search for clues for an architecture that derives from an engagement with the essential material resources on-site, and within the construction processes. Joyfully reusing that which might otherwise be deemed obsolete. Attempting to take part in a collective effort to foster a sustainable and long-lasting architecture, founded upon the necessary, the pragmatic, the constructed.

1 — Meyer, Ole, *De Tavse Bygninger*, Copenhagen: Aristo, 2000, p. 18.

Six short photo-essays

Søren Johansen, Sebastian Skovsted

Tipperne Bird Sanctuary, Denmark, October 2012 - February 2017

Fuglepolde, first visit

Nørrerad, first visit

Østerrad, first visit

New pond by birdhide, Storetipper

Landscape

Observing the desolate, flat landscape of the Tipperne peninsula, the marshes appear to stretch endlessly in all directions towards the horizon, where the sky asserts itself completely. Whether wandering in the Øster Rads beach meadows or trudging through the knee-deep waters of Tippesand, clad in waders, the landscape — almost entirely devoid of shadows, with the corresponding diffuse light from the sky — assumes a monotonous, atmospheric character. Uniformity lets nuances stand out. Changes in the light intensity, the shifting of the wind, a sudden heavy rain shower that disappears just as quickly as it arrived, the sun breaking through the cloud cover: this landscape possesses a unique transience, and constantly appears in a new state. This monotony and transience are why this landscape is quite so magnificent.

Vesterrad, first visit

Opgrøden, first visit

Bird hide, Storetipper

Pond, ochre sedimentation, Nørrerad, first visit

Four columns, Three Gorges Dam

Scaffolding, Chongqing

Leftover structures, Taipingxi

Sports field, Suzhou

Silent structures

Travelling through China, observing a country in a state of change. Gigantic building sites in various stages — some still in progress, others halted, abandoned, or nearly completed. Four pillars from a bridge that was never finished? Nets stretched over open fields. An endlessly empty billboard made of undulating aluminium panels, or is it a wall? A closed concrete box in the middle of a city. Incidental and silent structures, which have a beauty in their indifference and dedication to purpose. The seemingly arbitrary, the uncomposed, the disconcerting sense of lost functions and altered elements. Unintentional patterns, lightness, the partially demolished, and the unfinished.

Sports field, Beijing

Rooftop, Shanghai

Empty billboard, Beijing

Building with no openings, Nanjing

Six short photo-essays – **Søren Johansen, Sebastian Skovsted**

Carl C factory, Skjern, Denmark, November 2012 - May 2017

Steel pylon, first factory visit

Tipperne Tower, sections under production

Template

Tipperne Tower, sections under production

Production 1

Carl C factory is a producer of steel pylons made of round solid iron bars. Slender structures spread out in the landscape, providing mounting points for telecom installations. They are fragile yet robust structures; their lightness comes from their reflections on rounded surfaces and structural precision in their use of materials. A perhaps-unintended responsiveness to the sky. A laser cutter transforms a 25 mm plate into exact components, including holes for bolts. A template ensures that the threaded rods, cast into the foundation, will fit the base of the structure when mounted on-site. The dimensions of the galvanisation tubs define the size of the welded sections. Providing a possible rhythm of structure, repetition, and ways of assembly. The factory builds for cost effectiveness, using tried and proven technologies, with machines and methods for bending, cutting, drilling, welding.

Tipperne Tower, sliding doors under production

Tipperne Tower, pieces stored outside the factory

Tipperne Tower, sections under production

Tipperne Tower, pieces stored outside the factory

Binders

Layers added

Elements on flatbed truck

Concrete detailing before cladding

Construction site 1

When observing the many building sites of concrete-element structures (found throughout the country) in the process of being collected or clad in their final façade, they appear homogeneous due to their continuous tone and materiality, and yet they are rich in details and facets. A tactility is present in the top surface of the casting form's imperfections; it has small air bubbles, a shiny and uneven surface. A rough assembly of elements and floor slabs, the rhythm of binders and decorative ornamentation of cast-in-place steel brackets for mounting load-bearing exterior elements. Cast consoles, columns and reinforcements. Castings around window openings and shifting layers of casting create a sense of spatial depth. All these features will be covered up when the building is completed.

Cast window and door frames

Cast-in steel brackets

Walls stabilised by floor slab

Rhythm

Six short photo-essays – **Søren Johansen, Sebastian Skovsted**

Formwork, stored

CODAN, formwork with retarder oil

Various steel bars for reinforcement

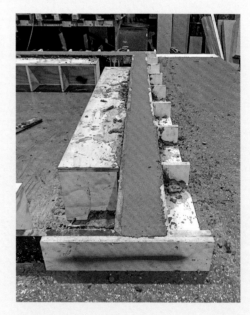

Formwork with concrete

Production 2

The production of prefabricated concrete elements is highly systematised, though specifically produced for each building and adapted and customised in various ways. Generic moulds and forms are used, and slightly more specific forms are cut and prepared in the carpentry workshop. Built by hand, in an industrialised setting. Reinforcement, connectors, openings, etc., are placed in the mould on the casting table. Typically, the front side is placed against the casting table for a smooth finish. If a retarder oil is added to the formwork, the cement will not harden and can be washed away to leave the aggregate visible. The top surfaces of the castings are roughly smoothed, with visible rotating circular grooves as a result. The dominance of prefabricated concrete elements stems from the industrialisation of the 1960s, which defined the skillset of the construction sector's workforce, national norms and legislation, as well as material supply lines.

Concrete poured into formwork

CODAN, first mock-up

Top of casting being smoothed

CODAN, element stored outside the factory

Foundation and plinth

Mounting wall element

Joining steel brackets and structure
© Rasmus Norlander

Intermediate spatiality

Construction site 2

The foundation traces the plan in the landscape. Observing the building taking form, it awaits the arrival of the elements at the construction site. In a short time, non-permanent spatialities arise, as temporary shoring posts and openings blend spaces while boundaries of "inside" and "outside" become fluid. Skylights, permanently designed, merge with areas open to the sky, where the roof slabs have not yet been placed. Two seemingly "identical" elements stand, yet one is assembled incorrectly — one with a door opening, the other without. A new opening is cut, while the other is sealed with the leftover block. Finished surfaces, without further material addition. In contrast to this, lightweight partitions are constructed on-site. A set of components assembled for the first time.

Permanent surfaces
© Rasmus Norlander

Opening cut, opening sealed

Temporary shoring posts

Light partitions

Biography
Johansen Skovsted

Johansen Skovsted Arkitekter is an architectural office based in Copenhagen, founded by **Søren Johansen** (1981) and **Sebastian Skovsted** (1982) in 2014. They both studied at the Royal Danish Academy, where they also taught from 2015 to 2021. They have lectured at institutions such as ETH Zurich, The Barbican, London Metropolitan University, Porto School of Architecture, the Oslo School of Architecture and Design, the University of New South Wales and the Sydney Opera House. In 2019, they ran a studio at the Porto Academy.

The office has won several prizes, such as the Dreyer Foundation's Honorary Award (2022), the Utzon Statuette (2021), the Nykredit Foundation's Motivation Prize (2021), the Häuser Award - Interior Prize (2020), the AD Design Award (2018), the Three-Year Working Grant by the Danish Arts Foundation (2017), the Danish Crown Prince Couple's Stardust Award (2016) and the Bisballe Prize (2015).

Collaborators (2014-23)

Niklas Lindelöw, Sofie Emilie Boye Kjær, Léo Duyck, Gustav Sigvant, Lauritz Wagn Møller, Josefine Jargil Årman, Anne Marie Stahl, Anders Normann, Jens Rudolf Ugelstad, Majse Marie Nørhald, Cecilie Morsbøl, Julius Wolff, Linn Granlund, Sebastian Zapata Ottung Henriksen, Amalie Skjellerup Bang, Emilie Møller Jensen, Melanie Schroff, Klara Lyshøj, Cecilie Riis Solberg, Olivia Ane Frey, Lisa Petersen, Camilla Vignola, Bjørn Lysgaard Pløger, Nick Cole, Frans Maurits Ahlbom, Francis Naydler, Panuela Aasted, Joel Brynielsson, Alexander Awramenko, Natalie Stas, Mikkel Breien Haugen, Sophie Nimb, Anne Sofie Kristensen, Panwaad Sai Chawalitanont, Anna Rosendahl, Victor Perlheden, Astrid Nanna Krabbe Høyer Simonsen, Maria Kristoffersen, Thomas Stefani, Lukasz Pita, Sixten Ditlefsen and Phoebe Cowen.